The plight of the younger generation, and the challenges this poses to inter-generational relationships, is a key issue for contemporary society. In this timely and fascinating book, two very experienced researchers tackle this central issue head-on. Using evidence from their own studies with middle class parents and their student/graduate children, we are given new insights into the realities of juggling finances and in/dependencies between the generations over time, providing an interesting account of the resulting dilemmas and tensions. This important book should be key reading for policy makers and politicians, as well as parents and young people, along with youth and family studies scholars, and anyone concerned with the future of younger generations.

Jane Ribbens McCarthy, *Visiting Professor, University of Reading; Reader in Family Studies (retired) and Visiting Fellow, Open University*

"Helicopter Parenting" and "Boomerang Children"

Drawing an unfavourable contrast between the position of students and graduates with that of their baby boomer parents has become a staple for media comment. Indeed, student indebtedness and difficulties in finding graduate jobs and housing typically contrasts markedly with their parents' experiences.

Broadening the investigation, *"Helicopter Parenting" and "Boomerang Children"* depicts how students and graduates are now more likely to be close to their parents, receive considerable financial and emotional support from them and, upon graduation, return home. Using qualitative data from two interview studies of middle-class families, this title explores the impact of these changes on young people's transition to independence and adulthood and on intergenerational and intragenerational equality.

This enlightening monograph will appeal to undergraduate and postgraduate students interested in fields such as Social Policy, Family Sociology and Education.

Anne West is Professor of Education Policy, London School of Economics and Political Science, UK.

Jane Lewis is Emeritus Professor of Social Policy, London School of Economics and Political Science, UK.

Routledge Advances in Sociology

For a full list of titles in this series, please visit www.routledge.com/series/SE0511

"Helicopter Parenting" and "Boomerang Children"

How Parents Support and Relate to Their Student and Co-Resident Graduate Children

Anne West and Jane Lewis

Routledge
Taylor & Francis Group

LONDON AND NEW YORK

First published 2018 by Routledge

2 Park Square, Milton Park, Abingdon, Oxfordshire OX14 4RN

52 Vanderbilt Avenue, New York, NY 10017

Routledge is an imprint of the Taylor & Francis Group, an informa business

First issued in paperback 2019

British Library Cataloguing-in-Publication Data
A catalogue record for this book is available from the British
Library

Library of Congress Cataloging-in-Publication Data
A catalog record for this book has been requested

ISBN: 978-1-138-68154-5 (hbk)
ISBN: 978-0-367-87849-8 (pbk)

Typeset in Times New Roman
by Apex CoVantage, LLC

Contents

Acknowledgements

We are grateful to the Leverhulme Trust (grant RPG-336) for financial support, to Dr Philip Noden and Dr Jonathan Roberts for research assistance, to the universities that assisted us, and to the parents, students and graduates who participated in the research.

This book is derived in part from the following articles:

Lewis, J. and West, A. Intergenerational relations between English students, graduates living at home, and their parents. *Social Policy and Administration.* First published 26 April 2016. © 2016 John Wiley & Sons Ltd. doi: *https://doi.org/10.1111/spol.12229.* Reprinted by permission of Wiley.

West, A., Lewis, J., Roberts, J. and Noden, P. Young adult graduates living in the parental home: Expectations, negotiations and parental financial support. *Journal of Family Issues.* First published December 2017. © Authors 2017. doi: *https://doi.org/10.1177/0192513X16643745.* Reprinted by permission of SAGE Publications.

Lewis, J., West, A. Roberts, J. and Noden, P. (2017). The experience of co-residence: Young adults returning to the parental home after graduation in England. *Families, Relationships and Societies,* 5(2): 247–262. © Policy Press 2016. doi: *https://doi.org/10.1332/2046743 15X14309191424695.* Reprinted by permission of Policy Press.

Lewis, J., West, A. Roberts, J. and Noden, P. (2015). Parents' involvement and university students' independence. *Families, Relationships and Societies,* 4(3): 417–432. © Policy Press 2015. doi: *https://doi.org/10.1332/ 204674314X14018716992515.* Reprinted by permission of Policy Press.

West, A., Roberts, J, Lewis, J. and Noden, P. (2015). Paying for higher education in England: Funding policy and families. *British Journal of Educational Studies,* 63(1): 23–45. © 2014 Taylor and Francis. doi: *http://dx.doi.org/10.1080/00071005.2014.990353.* Reprinted by permission of Taylor and Francis.

Introduction

Overview

The position of "young adults" is at the forefront of the debate about inter-generational equity, equality and fairness. In particular, their situation in relation to key indicators such as lack of affordable housing, shortage of "graduate jobs" and increasing student loan debt has raised, for the first time since World War II, the issue as to whether young people will do as well over the course of their adult lives as their parents have done.

The problems young adults face may mean that they fall back on parental financial and emotional support. In the case of middle-class students and recent graduates, who are the focus of this book, parents may help in alleviating the burden of student loan debt, managing their children's everyday lives and, on graduation, providing shelter in the form of the parental home and continued emotional, practical and financial help.

The majority of university undergraduate students in England live away from home[1] and many return home after graduating. As intergenerational fairness in relation to social policies has become less apparent – particularly regarding the introduction of increasingly high levels of student tuition fees – families have, where possible, felt the need to do more to support their children. While return to the parental home after graduation is accepted by both parents and children, there is little understanding as how best to manage another period of co-residence.

The students and graduates interviewed for this book attended predominantly older, élite English universities and, given the more advantaged socio-economic composition of those institutions, might be expected to be more likely to be able to rely on family support than groups of young adults at other higher education institutions. We focus on the nature of these young people's relationships with their families and the support they receive, for families are being increasingly called upon, and expected, to cushion the structural problems that their young adult children face. But this is not unproblematic in that first, not all young people have parents who can help; and second, the process of extended reliance on parents is likely to delay significantly the achievement of full adult independence. Parents appear to be more involved with their young adult children than has been the case for previous generations, with the label "helicopter parents" having been coined to describe parents who show 'a helicopter-like tendency to hover over children and swoop in to rescue them at the first sign of trouble' (Almendrala, 2015: 1).

We look first at the wider debate on intergenerational equity and the way in which attention has been drawn to the inferior position of young adults compared to that enjoyed by their parents, together with the implications of these ideas about intergenerational unfairness for potential conflict. Because education has become prolonged, and housing and graduate jobs hard to get, the transition to adulthood has over the decades become longer and less linear (Furstenbeg et al., 2004; Leccardi, 2016). Second, we look at intergenerational relations at the societal (macro-) level and family (micro-) level. Third, we turn to our own research studies. We review research on the transition to adulthood and independence along with work on parent/young adult relationships. We then describe the context for our two studies and the methods we adopted. Our focus is on the household level and what happens between parents and their student children living away from the parental home; and parents and their children who return home following university, often referred to as "boomerang" children.

Intergenerational equity

Generational inequalities and the potential for conflict became an issue for public debate in the USA in the 1980s, when the burden of public spending on pensions and health care for older people was highlighted (Binstock, 1994; Walker, 1996). Older people were typically characterised as a homogenous, self-interested and unproductive group, draining the resources of the generation below them. Inequalities between adults of working age and older people were not as strong a feature of the UK debate until much more recently.

Since the financial crisis of 2007–09, more attention has been paid to the position (and life-cycle prospects) of young adults in the UK, which has been contrasted unfavourably to the position of older people. In short, Hills et al. (2015) have shown that young people in their 20s, despite higher qualifications than any earlier generation, "lost out" between 2006–08 and 2013 in terms of jobs, hourly wages and weekly earnings, and assets, compared with those aged 55–64.

Politicians and commentators have stressed growing intergenerational inequalities (Howker and Malik, 2010; Willetts, 2010), often emphasising the greater political power exercised by the older, large "baby boom" generation (Willetts, 2010; see also Berry, 2014), and its selfishness. For White (2013) "generationalism" acts as a moral language to identify and seek rectification of injustice. Baby boomers are evoked as an interest-group able to shape the outcomes of elections by lobbying, and the young as victims. Generational thinking is popular because there are political dividends – with the prospect of intergenerational conflict being invoked to justify austerity and trimming the welfare state.

In recent literature on intergenerational conflict, the baby boom generation has been identified as the "villain of the piece" (Bristow, 2015). There is little agreement on who the baby boomers are – for Willetts (2010) they were those born between 1945 and 1965, and for Beckett (2010) those born between 1945 and 1955. However, Evandrou (1997) pointed out that there were two waves of baby boom births: the first wave (1946–1950) were born in a period of post-war austerity, but entered the labour market during a period of relative prosperity; the second wave (1961–1965) were born during a period of prosperity, but entered the labour market in a period of economic recession. Given the influence of formative experiences on shaping adult views, these differences mean that baby boomers cannot be seen as a homogenous group. Indeed, for individuals, the differences in the net lifetime effects of the "welfare" that results from their income levels, gender and family circumstances are more important than their date of birth (Hills, 1995).

The UK, like most Western countries, has an ageing population, and the baby boomers – however defined – are a large generation. It follows that their increasing longevity will make substantial demands on the welfare system, particularly health and social care services. Nevertheless, a recent review of social attitudes has concluded that there remains considerable evidence of cross-generational solidarity beyond the family context (Duffy et al., 2013) in respect of support for generation-specific benefits like pensions. Nor is there any sign of a diminution in informal family care by people of working age for their parents, which given the squeeze on social care budgets is likely to become yet more important (Pickard, 2015).

But intergenerational cash transfers also take place in the private sphere of the family. American sociological and psychological research has sought to show the extent of family solidarity in the face of fears about family conflict and decline (e.g., Bengtson, 1993). Fingerman et al. (2012a: 206) have commented that: 'Although the demise of the American family has been lamented throughout the Baby Boomers' lives, most Baby Boomers are actively involved with members of generations above and below them', and European research has shown that while the direction of cash flow in the public sphere is broadly upwards, the reverse is the case with cash transfers in the family (Kohli, 1999). Yet, while we know a considerable amount about the relationship between adults of working age and older people, we know relatively little about the nature of relationships between young adults and their parents.

Several issues have had a marked impact on families and their young adult children. While in the US tuition fees have long been charged by universities, in England their introduction was more recent. The resultant graduate debt along with changes to the structure of the housing and labour markets has had an impact on families. Privatisation has multiple meanings and takes many forms (Starr, 1988), but one of the most important is the "great risk shift" away from the state and toward the private sphere of the family (Antonucci, 2016; Hacker, 2006). However, the shift from state to individual responsibility has in practice been a shift to families wherever parents are willing and able to offer financial support. In a similar vein, the effects of the 2007–09 recession on graduate employment have prolonged graduates' dependence on parents, again where they are willing and able.

Intergenerational relations at the macro- and micro-levels

For Willetts (2010), the macro-level intergenerational contract grew out of the support family members of different ages give to each other on a reciprocal basis. However, as Walker (1996) has pointed out in respect of the obligation to care for older family members, the micro-level intergenerational contract between family members is a delicate balance between reciprocity, affection and duty (see also Künemund, 2008), something that may also hold true for young adults returning home. The relationship between the intergenerational contracts at the macro- and micro-levels is a crucial dimension of the debate over the pursuit of greater intergenerational fairness.

Macro-level fairness

Contributors to the debate about intergenerational fairness agree that some notion of an intergenerational contract underpins intergenerational transfers made by welfare states, which act as (compulsory) savings banks and redistribute resources between different people (Barr, 2001). The savings bank function depends on a level of trust in social policies; this has become more fragile as policies, such as the financing of higher education, have become ever more subject to reforms that transfer more responsibility for provision onto individual recipients and/or their families. Furthermore, the plea by many commentators, fearful of intergenerational conflict, to treat generations equally in the sense of "the same" ignores what has hitherto been a correct assumption – namely, that there will be economic growth and that future generations will be better off (Piachaud et al., 2009).

While there is evidence of considerable intergenerational solidarity (Duffy et al., 2013), this may diminish in face of both policy change and structural change in housing and labour markets. Economists have established that those born in Great Britain in the early 1980s started employment on incomes that were no higher than those born in the previous decade – the first cohort since World War II not to start working-age life with higher incomes than their predecessors at the same age. This is because the 2007–09 recession hit the pay and employment of young adults the hardest. Furthermore the cohort born in the early 1980s had accumulated less wealth than their predecessors had by the same age, and had much lower home-ownership rates in early adulthood than any other post-war cohort (Cribb et al., 2016).

Sociologists in the UK have explored the structural changes that have taken place and their consequences, for example, the extent to which the introduction of tuition fees and loans has resulted in many middle-class parents providing significant financial support to their student children (e.g., Ahier, 2000), and the high proportion of graduates returning to the parental home because of the difficulty experienced in finding both a graduate job and an affordable place to live (e.g., Berrington et al., 2013; Sage et al., 2013). House building has not kept up with demographic change, resulting in a decreased supply of housing (Pennington et al., 2012). At the same time, precarious employment has increased and even though having a degree is key to avoiding such work, graduates may go into precarious jobs – which generally offer low wages and limited prospects – at least on a temporary basis before they obtain a well-paid, stable job (Berrington et al., 2017).

Micro-level fairness

For Bengtson (1993) there is a "contract" in terms of informal expectations and obligations that creates solidarity or conflict and which has to be negotiated in everyday life. He argues that family-based micro-level generational obligations and exchanges have remained relatively similar over time, while issues of macro-level age group reciprocities and equities have not (population ageing, the level of social welfare provision). Those making the case for intergenerational unfairness use cross-sectional data and ignore life course reciprocity. Bengtson also calls attention to the squeeze on the middle generation (often called the "sandwich generation" – responding to the needs of both adult children and older parents). It is noteworthy that Fingerman et al. (2012a) find baby boomers are more often involved with their children than ageing parents. Willetts (2010) explicitly gives primacy to family support over that provided by the state. More recently there has been evidence of strong financial and material support by parents for young adults, both as students and as graduates in their 20s (Heath and Calvert, 2013). This is in contrast to the situation in the past. As Furstenberg et al. (2004: 40), writing about the US, note:

> A century ago . . . young adults typically helped their parents when they first went to work, if (as was common) they still lived with their parents. Now, many young adults continue to receive support from their parents even after they begin working.

However, the extent to which the aid given by family members to each other constitutes an effective alternative to state provision is debatable.

In some areas, such as higher education, the role of families has long been important in both the US and in the UK. In England the introduction of high tuition fees – albeit supported by government loans – has resulted in graduates accruing high levels of debt. Indeed English graduates face some of the highest debts internationally – even though the repayment system is income-contingent and relatively simple compared to that in the US (Kirby, 2016). As regards housing, Gardiner (2016) notes that families themselves often step in, using private intergenerational transfers, to ameliorate the worst effects of housing scarcity. The Council of Mortgage Lenders (2015) estimated that in 2014, just over half of first-time buyers were likely to have bought a property with family assistance; and Legal and General (2016) found that in 2016, a quarter of all homeowners received help – mostly from parents via a gift – when they bought the home they lived in. Furthermore, material support has often been accompanied by greater parental involvement with young children and the offer of emotional support of various kinds: encouragement, advice and a "listening ear" (e.g., Scabini et al., 2006).

The motivation of family members is generally agreed by sociologists to stem from norms of responsibility or obligation, ideas about reciprocity, and intimacy or affection. Künemund and Rein (1999) concluded that norms of responsibility are less stable than norms of reciprocity. However, Finch and Mason (1993) argued that all these motivations to help other family members may operate together (see also Künemund, 2008). Thus the obligation to give help is conceptualised as a result of a process of negotiation that balances out giving and receiving, one kind of assistance against another, independence and interdependence. For economists, altruism and exchange are the two possible motivations, with altruism assuming a moral duty or obligation, and exchange theory proposing that giving to others is motivated by the expectation that they will reciprocate (Künemund, 2008). But models of altruism and exchange are not able to capture the complexity of the motives of individuals revealed by the sociological studies. The balance between reciprocity, affection and obligation in respect of family support is likely to be delicate, and hard to negotiate over time.

Research has emphasised the crucial role played by families and how this is a source of intragenerational inequality, with some parents being able to support their children and others less able to do so (Settersten and Ray, 2010). Swartz et al. (2011: 427), focusing on housing and financial assistance, have argued that 'families are absorbing some of the problems associated with an economy that requires more education but offers less stable employment and lower wages for young people'. Newman (2012: 196) sees the family as a 'buffer' and for the middle class it 'represents both a haven in the heartless world of market pressures and a springboard to a more prestigious future'. We suggest that the balance between public and private (in the sense of familial) provision is fragile, and that tilting the balance towards the family is as (or more) likely to exacerbate the issue of *intra*generational as intergenerational inequality.

Our research: parents, students and co-resident graduates

The two research studies we report in this book bring together issues at the macro- and micro-levels. Our first study focuses on parents and their student children studying at university and living away from home; and the second on parents and their co-resident graduate children. The issue of independence is key to both studies, albeit that the understandings of students, graduates and parents differ, and those of the young adults were at times more in line with definitions of autonomy. In the next section, we discuss research relating to independence, the transition to adulthood and, related to both, the nature of parent/young adult relationships. We then outline the specific contexts and methods of each study.

Literature on transitions, independence and parent/young adult relationships

One of the main tasks of the Western family has been seen as "launching the child" – ensuring she or he can think and act independently (Parsons and Bales, 1955). In this context, two issues are of particular relevance, namely what constitutes independence and does more parental support delay independence? Sociologists and psychologists agree that the transition to adulthood has changed in recent decades. Sociologists have argued that the period of "young adulthood" has become "destandardised" (e.g., Leccardi, 2016). As Côté (2000: 5) noted, it is 'becoming more hazardous' and 'the destination is becoming more difficult to reach', while for Newman (2012: 1), adulthood has become 'slippery'. Some of the traditional markers – job, home, marriage, children – may not appear at all. Thus, Furstenberg et al. (2004) reported that the most important milestones for achieving adulthood in 2002 amongst a representative sample of American adults aged 18 and over, were completing education (97 per cent), being financially independent (97 per cent) and being employed full-time (96 per cent).

Psychologists have focused on young people's conceptions of the transition to adulthood. In one study, Arnett (2001) found that the most frequently endorsed items (ranging from 93 per cent to 72 per cent) in a questionnaire administered to 20- to 29-year-olds (or "emerging adults") were all on a subscale relating to individualism – accepting responsibility for the consequences of one's actions; deciding on personal beliefs and values independently of parents or other influences; establishing a relationship with parents as an equal adult; and being financially independent from parents. These are also related to the extent to which students are able to break free of supervision by parents – what the media have termed "helicopter" parents – and how far graduates who are once again co-resident with their parents – in the manner of "boomerang" children – can establish a relationship with their parents as equal adults.

Psychologists argue that the transition has become more volitional (Arnett, 2001; Scabini et al., 2006) and the importance of 'feeling' adult, not merely 'being' adult, has also been stressed (Mary, 2014: 424). Sociologists argue that cultural and economic factors have played a crucial role in slowing and changing the path to adulthood (Settersten and Ray, 2010; Newman, 2012). Associated with both psychological and sociological ideas about adulthood are the concepts of independence and autonomy. Young people who are not fully autonomous or independent have been described as being semi-autonomous (Goldscheider and DaVanzo, 1985), semi-dependent (Ahier and Moore, 1999; Antonucci, 2016), or 'not quite adults' (Settersten and Ray, 2010: 201).

Some authors use the terms autonomy and independence synonymously. However, Gaudet (2001) uses the former to mean the ability to make decisions for oneself; and for Wintre and Yaffe (2000: 16) a sense of autonomy is informed by three components: self-reliance, a 'healthy' sense of identity, and work orientation. For Cicchelli and Martin (2004: 621), autonomy may encompass self-reliance in one domain alongside dependence in another. Turning to independence, Manzoni (2016: 371), using quantitative analysis, has demonstrated that this is a multi-dimensional concept comprising living arrangements, earnings, financial support, self-perceived independence, and the sense of being an adult. Qualitative research has found, first, that young people and parents may have different understandings of independence and sometimes these may more closely resemble definitions of autonomy than independence; and second, that parents can help their children develop skills to become more independent (see Gillies et al., 2001).

Whether more structural indicators of independence (see Furstenberg et al., 2004; Settersten and Ray, 2010) are used, more individualistic ones (see Arnett, 2001), or a combination of these (Manzoni, 2016), it is important to note both the range of dimensions and also the extent to which "money" is central to most of them. For this reason, in the empirical chapters that follow (Chapters 1 to 4), we have separated consideration of financial arrangements from other forms of support.

Turning to the relationship between parents and young adult children, the literature is divided on how far closer relationships might encourage dependence rather than independence. Considerable attention has focused on students in this regard, and on a new form of "intensive", "overparenting", or "helicopter parenting" (Fingerman et al., 2012b). Levine and Dean (2012) surveyed American senior student affairs officers and students, and reported at length on inappropriate interventions, which included a parent demanding to spend the night with his son in a hall of residence for the first week of term and a parent inspecting the son's room regularly to make sure it was clean. They also showed the extent to which students were likely to treat the parent as the "first port of call", for example in the case of a student calling a parent when stuck in a lift, despite the number to call in emergencies being clearly posted (see also Coburn, 2006). These examples are at the high end of the "parental intervention" scale, although it seems that large numbers of American university administrators have experienced something of this kind. Such intensive or overparenting may result in lower levels of autonomy, competence and family satisfaction (Segrin et al., 2012; Schiffrin et al., 2014). But studies have also found positive effects, including better adjustment to university (e.g., Fingerman et al., 2012b; Wintre and Yaffe, 2000). Others have pointed out that "parental autonomy support" – the promotion of independent functioning and/or encouragement of the young person to follow his or her true personal interests and values – may be related to well-being (Soenens et al., 2007).

In the case of the "boomerang" graduates returning to the parental home, parents often remain the main source of emotional support and practical advice, as well as money, but the literature is more likely to see the relationship in terms of a "joint enterprise" (Scabini et al., 2006; Swartz et al., 2011) designed to enable young adults to develop skills, gain experience and attain the shared goal of full independence. Still, return to the parental home may be construed differently by the graduate and by the parent: Roberts et al. (2016) found that living in the parental home served different functions from the perspective of the co-resident graduate. The main issues for this group are the nature of the parent/child relationship, and how this relationship fosters or otherwise the achievement of full independence. Research indicates that *how* the return is managed, and whether the parent succeeds in supporting autonomy rather than engaging in directive, controlling behaviours, is crucial (e.g., Soenens et al., 2007).

Focus of our studies

The focus in our two studies, which were carried out in 2012 and 2013, is on the generation commonly referred to as "Millennials". They are variously defined, but for the Resolution Foundation (Gardiner, 2016) they are those born between 1981 and 2000 and for the Pew Centre those born between 1981 and 1997 (Fry, 2016). The students in our first study – on parents and students living away from home – were born in the early-1990s, and the graduates in our second study – on parents and co-resident graduates – were born between the mid-1980s and the early-1990s. The focus in both studies was on middle-class families, a generally under-researched group in the UK and the US (but see Brooks, 2003; Napolitano et al., 2014). In both studies, parents and children agreed to be interviewed, so we would expect a relatively low level of tension.

Study on parents and students living away from home

Background

Higher education in England was until relatively recently restricted to a minority of the population. In 1970 for example, participation by school leavers was around 8 per cent. There was a rapid expansion during the 1990s and it reached 24 per cent in 2012 (Bolton, 2012; Department for Business, Innovation and Skills, 2014). While the expansion has been across all social classes, the proportion of young people from middle-class backgrounds remains much higher than that from working-class backgrounds – in 2013–14 it was 52 per cent versus 27 per cent (Higher Education Statistics Agency, 2015). Indeed, for middle-class children higher education has become 'not just an expectation but a rite of passage in the transition to adult life' (Bathmaker et al., 2016: 145). Higher education is stratified, with older, traditional universities (established before 1992) generally catering for more advantaged students than universities established since 1992 (commonly referred to as "new" universities).

Going away to university has long been seen as a marker along the road to fully independent living and is the norm in England – with just over 70 per cent of students living away from the parental home (UK House of Commons, 2013), although as Holdsworth (2009) has observed, going away to university has been a largely élite practice. Given our interest in middle-class families, we focused on students attending older, traditional universities.

The parents in our sample had paid no tuition fees to attend British universities and as students, almost all had received means-tested government maintenance grants to cover the costs of living away from the parental home. For students in our study, loans had largely replaced grants, and tuition fees – of around £3,000 per annum – were levied by English universities.

We adopted a qualitative approach in order to probe the nature of parents' financial help to student children and also to comment on the debate about the effects of parents' emotional support and involvement on their student children's progress towards independence. The term "helicopter parents" was coined in the US to describe the behaviour of parents who keep a close eye on their student offspring, hovering, ready to intervene at the first sign of difficulty. Indeed, Wartman and Savage (2008: 1) have noted a 'new level of family involvement', which does not fit with the personal history of today's educators. Nor does it fit, for the most part, with parents' own experience of going away to university.

Methods

Our sample comprised undergraduate students at two long-established English universities, and their parents. We recruited 14 students and their parents from one university, and 15 students and parents from the other, carrying out 58 interviewees in total. Students and parents were interviewed separately. The students had nearly or recently completed the first year of studies and were living away from home during term-time, having previously – whilst at school – lived in the family home. In 22 cases mothers were interviewed, in six cases fathers and in one case both parents were interviewed (that is, 29 interviews with 30 parents). We interviewed 20 female and nine male students. A majority of interviewees in our study were female, which is not unusual in research focusing on students and their parents (see David et al., 2003).

Most qualitative research has focused on the views of students, but Cullaty (2011) recommended that future studies should look at parents: in our study we sought views of both parents and their student children. All but three of the students in our study were from professional or managerial family backgrounds and virtually all the parents we interviewed had graduated from British universities. Twenty-three parents were White British; the remainder were of Dutch, Irish, South African, Turkish, Irish/American (one of each) and Indian (two) origin. Twenty parents were married, seven divorced and two widowed.[2]

We asked our interviewees about a range of different issues regarding the extent to which parents contributed to tuition fees and living costs, and students' perceptions of financial independence (see Chapter 1); the kind of contact parents had with their student children, who instigated contact, how often, by what means and for what purpose; whether the student turned to the parent for emotional support or help with day-to-day living; and developing independence (see Chapter 2).

Study of parents and co-resident graduates

Background

The age at which young people leave the parental home varies between countries. Across Europe, young people leave the parental home earliest in the Nordic countries and latest in southern and eastern European countries. Thus, in 2011, 50 per cent of young people left home at the age of 20 in Denmark, compared with 23 in France and Germany, 24 in the UK, 29 in Greece and 30 in Bulgaria (Eurofound, 2014).

In the UK in 2016, 25 per cent of 20- to 34-year-olds were living with their parents – an increase of 4 percentage points since 1996 (Office for National Statistics, 2016). Finishing full-time higher education has been found to be one of the main reasons for returning home across socio-economic groups for both men and women (Berrington et al., 2012), and the increase has been particularly strong – at least among those in their 20s – for those from the wealthiest backgrounds (Berrington et al., 2017). Stone et al. (2011) found that half of graduates aged 22 and 24 in permanent, full-time employment lived with a parent. While recent graduates aged 21 to 30 years of age have had consistently higher unemployment rates than older graduates, the percentage working in a non-graduate (and generally lower paid) job has also increased since 2008–09 (ONS, 2012a). The increase in the number of young adults living in the parental home has also coincided with an increase in the average house price paid by first-time buyers of 40 per cent between 2002 and 2011 (ONS, 2012b).

A large body of mainly US quantitative work has explored the degree of satisfaction experienced by parents and young adults returning home (e.g.,

Aquilino, 1999; Pillemer and Suitor, 2002). Most of this work has explored intergenerational relationships on aggregate, although Holdsworth and Morgan (2005), who questioned Arnett's view of young adults "freely choosing" rather than reacting to or coping with structural change (see also Côté and Bynner, 2008), used qualitative data. Our approach is also qualitative and looks at the household level, for as Furstenberg (2010: 74) has commented: 'what happens inside families on a day-by-day basis . . . remains a largely unexplored topic'. In short, while return to the parental home after graduation has become more accepted by both parents and children, there is little understanding as to how parents and children may conduct themselves during another period of co-residence.

Methods

Interviewees for this study were approached through the alumni office of a long-established English university with an above-average representation of students from middle-class backgrounds. We carried out 54 semi-structured interviews separately with parents and co-resident graduate children. We interviewed 27 parents (17 mothers and ten fathers) and 27 graduate children living in the parental home.

Nineteen graduates were female and eight were male; they were between 21 and 29 years of age. Twenty were White British, four South Asian and three of mixed ethnicity (Asian/White British).[3] The graduates' backgrounds were predominantly middle class. Of those interviewed, 26 had at least one graduate parent and at least one parent who was – or had retired from – a professional or managerial occupation.[4] Again, a majority of interviewees were female. Young women are more likely to return to the parental home following graduation (Berrington et al., 2012); and they may also be more willing to participate than young men. In the case of parents, the higher proportion of mothers may be related to the role that they generally play in caring for their children (see David et al., 2003). Graduates had lived with their parents for between three months and seven and a half years. Importantly from the parents' point of view, all but one felt that they had a large enough house or flat to accommodate an adult child without undue difficulty.

We asked about the reasons for graduates returning to the parental home and how parents and young adult children felt about their situation, together with their day-to-day interactions and achieving independence (Chapter 3); we also explored the financial arrangements between parents and graduate children, including contributions to the household economy, and how parents sought to foster responsibility and financial independence in their young adult children (Chapter 4). The final chapter presents our concluding reflections.

Notes

1 In 2011–12, 70 per cent of English-domiciled students on full-time three-year undergraduate programmes (the normal duration of a degree course in England) lived away from home (UK House of Commons, 2013).
2 For more details of methods, see Lewis et al. (2015) and West et al. (2015).
3 See West et al. (2016) for more details of the methods.
4 Twenty-two graduates lived with their mother and father, one with her mother and stepfather, three with a single mother and one with a single father. There were 12 mother/daughter, five mother/son, seven father/daughter, and three father/son dyads.

References

Ahier, J. (2000). Financing higher education by loans and fees: Theorizing and researching the private effects of a public policy. *Journal of Education Policy*, 15(6): 683–700.
Ahier, J. and Moore, R. (1999). Post-16 education, semi-dependent youth and the privatisation of inter-age transfers: Re-theorising youth transition. *British Journal of Sociology of Education*, 20(4): 515–530.
Almendrala, A. (2015, September 30). 5 signs you were raised by helicopter parents and what to do about it. *Huffington Post*. Retrieved from: www.huff ingtonpost.com/entry/5-ways-to-tell-you-were-raised-by-helicopter-parents_ us_5609de6ee4b0dd850308e260
Antonucci, L. (2016). *Student Lives in Crisis: Deepening Inequality in Times of Austerity*. Bristol: Policy Press.
Aquilino, W. S. (1999). Two views of one relationship: Comparing parents' and young adult children's reports of the quality of intergenerational relations. *Journal of Marriage and Family*, 61(4): 858–870.
Arnett, J. J. (2001). Conceptions of the transition to adulthood: Perspectives from adolescence through midlife. *Journal of Adult Development*, 8(2): 133–143.
Barr, N. (2001). *The Welfare State as Piggy Bank: Information, Risk, Uncertainty and the Role of the State*. Oxford: Oxford University Press.
Bathmaker, A.-M., Ingram, N., Abrahams, J., Hoare, A., Waller, R. and Bradley, H. (2016). *Higher Education Social Class and Social Mobility Higher Education Social Class: The Degree Generation*. London: Palgrave Macmillan.
Beckett, F. (2010). *What Did the Baby Boomers Ever Do for Us?* London: Biteback Publishing.
Bengtson, V. L. (1993). Is the "contract across generations" changing? Effects of population aging on obligations and expectations across age groups'. In V. L. Bengtson and W. A. In V. L. Bengtson and W. A. Achenbaum (Eds.), *The changing Contract across Generations* (pp. 3–23). New York: Aldine de Gurgyer.
Berrington, A., Duta, A. and Wakeling, P. (2017). *Youth social citizenship and class inequalities in transitions to adulthood in the UK*. ESRC Centre for Population Change Working Paper No 81. Southampton: University of Southampton. Retrieved from: http://eprints.soton.ac.uk/405269/1/2017_WP81_Youth_social_ citizenship_Berrington_et_al.pdf

Berrington, A., Stone, J. and Falkingham, J. (2012). *Gender differences in returning to the parental home in the UK: The role of social policy*. Paper presented to the 10th European Social Policy Analysis Conference, Edinburgh.

Berrington, A., Stone, J. and Falkingham, J. (2013). *The impact of parental characteristics and contextual effects on returns to the parental home in Britain*. ESRC Centre for Population Change Working Paper No 29. Southampton: University of Southampton.

Berry, C. (2014). Young people and the ageing electorate: Breaking the unwritten rule of representative democracy. *Parliamentary Affairs*, 67(3): 708–725.

Binstock, R. H. (1994). Transcending intergenerational equity. In T. R. Marmor, T. M. Smeeding and V. L. Greene (Eds.), *Economic Security and Intergenerational Justice: A Look at North America* (pp. 156–163). Washington, DC: The Urban Institute Press.

Bolton, P. (2012). *Education: Historical Statistics SN/SG/4252*. London: House of Commons Library. Retrieved from: www.parliament.uk/briefing-papers/SN04252/education-historical-statistics.

Bristow, J. (2015). *Baby Boomers and Generational Conflict*. Basingstoke: Palgrave Macmillan.

Brooks, R. (2003). Young people's higher education choices: The role of family and friends. *British Journal of Sociology of Education*, 24(3): 283–297.

Cicchelli, V. and Martin, C. (2004). Young adults in France: Becoming adult in the context of increased autonomy and dependency. *Journal of Comparative Family Studies*, 35(4): 615–626.

Coburn, K. (2006, July/August). Organizing a ground crew for today's helicopter parents. *About Campus*, 9–16.

Côté, J. (2000). *Arrested Adulthood: The Changing Nature of Maturity and Identity*. New York: New Yok University Press.

Côté, J. and Bynner, J. M. (2008). Changes in the transition to adulthood in the UK and Canada: The role of structure and agency in emerging adulthood. *Journal of Youth Studies*, 11(3): 251–268.

Council of Mortgage Lenders. (2015, May 15). *New CML data shows nearly half of first-time buyers didn't use the 'bank of mum and dad'*. Retrieved from: www.cml.org.uk/news/news-and-views/712/

Cribb, J., Hood, A. and Joyce, R. (2016). *The Economic Circumstances of Different Generations: The Latest Picture*. London: Institute for Fiscal Studies.

Cullaty, B. (2011). The role of parental involvement in the autonomy development of traditional-age college students. *Journal of College Student Development*, 52(4): 25–439.

David, M. E., Ball, S. J., Davies, J. and Reay, D. (2003). Gender issues in parental involvement in student choices of higher education. *Gender and Education*, 15(1): 21–36.

Department for Business Innovation and Skills. (2014). *Participation rates in higher education: Academic years 2006/2007–2012/2013 (Provisional)*. Retrieved from: www.gov.uk/government/uploads/system/uploads/attachment_data/file/347864/HEIPR_PUBLICATION_2012-13.pdf

Duffy, B., Hall, S., O'Leary, D. and Pope, S. (2013). *Generation Strains: A Demos and Ipsos Mori Report on Changing Attitudes to Welfare*. London: Demos.

Eurofound. (2014). *Mapping youth transitions in Europe*. Luxembourg: Publications Office of the European Union. Retrieved from: www.jugendpolitikineuropa. de/downloads/4-20-3595/EF1392EN.pdf

Evandrou, M. (1997). Introduction. In M. Evandrou (Ed.), *Baby Boomers. Ageing in the 21st Century* (pp. 8–14). London: Age Concern England.

Finch, J. and Mason, J. (1993). *Negotiating Family Responsibilities*. London: Routledge.

Fingerman, K. L., Cheng, Y., Wesselmann, E. G., Zarit, S., Furstenberg, F. and Birditt, K. S. (2012b). Helicopter parents and landing pad kids: Intense parental support of grown children. *Journal of Marriage and Family*, 74: 880–896.

Fingerman, K. L., Pillemer, K. A., Silverstein, M. and Suitor, J. J. (2012a). The baby boomers' intergenerational relationships. *The Gerontologist*, 52(2): 199–209.

Fry, R. (2016, April 25). *Millennials overtake baby boomers as America's largest generation*. Pew Research Centre. Retrieved from: www.pewresearch.org/fact-tank/2016/04/25/millennials-overtake-baby-boomers/

Furstenberg, F. (2010). On a new schedule: Transitions to adulthood and family change. *The Future of Children*, 20(1): 67–87.

Furstenberg, F., Kennedy, S., McLoyd, V. C., Rumbaut, R. G. and Settersten, R. A. (2004). Growing up is harder to do. *Contexts*, 3(3): 33–41.

Gardiner, L. (2016). *Stagnation Generation. The Case for Renewing the Intergenerational Contract*. Resolution Foundation. Retrieved from: www.resolutionfoun dation.org/app/uploads/2016/06/Intergenerational-commission-launch-report.pdf

Gaudet, S. (2001). La responsabilité dans les débuts de l'âge adulte. *Lien social et Politiques*, 46(2): 71–83.

Gillies, V., Ribbens McCarthy, J. and Holland, J. (2001). *'Pulling Together, Pulling Apart': The Family Lives of Young People*. London: Family Policy Studies Centre for Joseph Rowntree Foundation.

Goldscheider, F. and DaVanzo, J. (1985). Living arrangements and the transition to adulthood. *Demography*, 22(4): 545–563.

Hacker, J. S. (2006). *The Great Risk Shift: The Assault on American Jobs, Families, Health Care and Retirement*. New York: Oxford University Press.

Heath, S. and Calvert, E. (2013). Gifts, loans and intergenerational support for young adults. *Sociology*, 47(6): 1120–1135.

Higher Education Statistics Agency. (2015, July 16). Personal communication.

Hills, J. (1995). The welfare state and redistribution between generations. In J. Falkingham and J. Hills (Eds.), *The Dynamic of Welfare: The Welfare State and the Life Cycle* (pp. 32–61). Hemel Hempstead: Harvester Wheatsheaf and Prentice Hall.

Hills, J., Cunliffe, J., Obolenskaya, P. and Karagiannaki, E. (2015). *Falling behind, getting ahead: The changing structure of inequality in the UK, 2007–2013*. Research Report 5. London: CASE, LSE. Retrieved from: http://sticerd.lse.ac.uk/dps/case/spcc/rr05.pdf

Holdsworth, C. (2009). 'Going away to uni': Mobility, modernity and independence of English higher education students. *Environment and Planning A*, 41: 1849–1864.

Holdsworth, C. and Morgan, D. (2005). *Transitions in Context Leaving Home, Independence and Adulthood*. Maidenhead: Open University Press.

Howker, E. and Malik, S. (2010). *Jilted Generation: How Britain Has Bankrupted Its Youth*. London: Icon Books. Retrieved from: www.un.org/en/development/desa/population/publications/pdf/expert/2011-10_Iacovou_Expert-paper.pdf

Kirby, P. (2016). *Degrees of Debt: Funding and Finance for Undergraduates in Anglophone Countries*. London: Sutton Trust. Retrieved from: www.suttontrust.com/wp-content/uploads/2016/04/DegreesofDebt.pdf

Kohli, M. (1999). Private and public transfers between generations: Linking the family and the state. *European Societies*, 1(1): 81–104.

Künemund, H. (2008). Intergenerational relations within the family and the state. In C. Saraceno (Ed.), *Families Ageing and Social Policy: Intergenerational Solidarity* (pp. 105–122). Cheltenham: Edward Elgar.

Künemund, H. and Rein, M. (1999). There is more to receiving than needing: Theoretical arguments and empirical explorations of crowding in and crowding out. *Ageing and Society*, 19(1): 93–121.

Leccardi, C. (2016). Facing uncertainty: Temporality and biographies in the new century. In C. Leccardi and E. Ruspini (Eds.), *A New Youth? Young People, Generations and Family Life* (pp. 1–14). London: Routledge. First edition (2006). Aldershot: Ashgate.

Legal and General. (2016). *The bank of mum and dad*. Retrieved from: www.legalandgeneral.com/_resources/pdfs/insurance/The-bank-of-mum-and-dad-full-report.PDF

Levine, A. and Dean, D. R. (2012). *Generation on a Tightrope: A Portrait of Today's College Student*. San Francisco, CA: Jossey-Bass.

Lewis, J., West, A., Roberts, J. and Noden, P. (2015). Parents' involvement and university students' independence. *Families, Relationships and Societies*, 4(3): 417–432.

Manzoni, A. (2016). Conceptualizing and measuring youth independence multidimensionally in the United States. *Acta Sociologica*, 59(4): 362–377.

Mary, A. A. (2014). Re-evaluating the concept of adulthood and the framework of transition. *Journal of Youth Studies*, 17(3): 415–429.

Napolitano, L. J., Pacholok, S. and Furstenberg, F. F. (2014). Educational aspirations, expectations and realities for middle-income families. *Journal of Family Issues*, 35: 1200–1226.

Newman, K. S. (2012). *The Accordion Family*. Boston, MA: Beacon Press.

Office for National Statistics (ONS). (2012a). *Graduates in the Labour Market, 2012*. London: ONS.

Office for National Statistics (ONS). (2012b). *Young Adults Living With Parents in the UK, 2011*. London: ONS.

Office for National Statistics (ONS). (2016). *Families and households in the UK: 2016*. Retrieved from: www.ons.gov.uk/peoplepopulationandcommunity/birthsdeathsandmarriages/families/bulletins/familiesandhouseholds/2016

Parsons, T. and Bales, R. F. (1955). *Family, Socialization and Interaction Process*. New York: Macmillan.

Pennington, J., Ben-Galim, D. and Cooke, G. (2012). *No Place to Call Home*. London: IPPR. Retrieved from: www.ippr.org/files/images/media/files/publica tion/2012/12/no-place-home_Dec2012_10017.pdf?noredirect=1

Piachaud, D., Macnicol, J. and Lewis, J. (2009). *Just Ageing? A Think Piece on Intergenerational Equity*. London: Equality and Human Rights Commission, Age Concern and Help the Aged.

Pickard, L. (2015). A growing care gap? The supply of unpaid care for older people by their adult children in England to 2032. *Ageing and Society*, 35: 96–123.

Pillemer, K. and Suitor, J. J. (2002). Explaining mothers' ambivalence towards their adult children. *Journal of Marriage and Family*, 64: 602–613.

Roberts, J., Noden, P., West, A. and Lewis, J. (2016). Living with the parents: The purpose of young graduates' return to the parental home in England. *Journal of Youth Studies*, 19(3): 319–337.

Sage, J., Evandrou, M. and Falkingham, J. (2013). Onwards or homewards? Complex graduate migration pathways, well-being, and the 'parental safety net'. *Population, Space and Place*, 19(6): 738–755.

Scabini, E., Marta, E. and Lanz, M. (2006). *The Transition to Adulthood and Family Relations*. Hove: Psychology Press.

Schiffrin, H. H., Liss, M., Miles-McLean, H., Geary, K. A., Erchull, M. J. and Tashner, T. (2014). Helping or hovering? The effects of helicopter parenting on college students' well-being. *Journal of Child and Family Studies*, 23: 548–557.

Segrin,C., Woszidlo, A., Givertz, M., Bauer, A. and Taylor Murphy, M. (2012). The association between overparenting, parent-child communication and entitlement and adaptive traits in adult children. *Family Relations*, 61: 237–252.

Settersten, R. and Ray, B. E. (2010). *Not Quite Adults*. New York: Random House.

Soenens, B., Vansteenkiste, M., Lens, W., Luyckx, K., Goossens, L., Byers, W. and Ryan, R. M. (2007). Conceptualizing parental autonomy support: Perceptions of promotion of independence versus promotion of volitional functioning. *Developmental Psychology*, 43(3): 633–646.

Starr, P. (1988). The meaning of privatization. *Yale Law and Policy Review*, 6(1): 6–41.

Stone, J., Berrington, A. and Falkingham, J. (2011). The changing determinants of UK young adults' living arrangements. *Demographic Research*, 25: 629–666.

Swartz, T. T., Kim, M., Uno, M., Mortimer, J. and O'Brien, K. (2011). Safety nets and scaffolds: Parental support in the transition to adulthood. *Journal of Marriage and Family*, 73: 414–429.

UK House of Commons. (2013, October 15). Written Answers, Hansard Vol. 568 col 684–685W.

Walker, A. (1996). Intergenerational relations and the provision of welfare. In A. Walker (Ed.), *The New Generational Contract: Intergenerational Relations, Old Age and Welfare* (pp. 10–36). London: UCL Press.

Wartman, K. and Savage, M. (2008). *Parental involvement in higher education: Understanding the relationship among students, parents and the institution*. Higher Education Report Series, 33, 6. San Francisco, CA: Association for the Study of Higher Education.

West, A., Lewis, J., Roberts, J. and Noden, P. (2016). Young adult graduates living in the parental home: Expectations, negotiations and parental financial support. *Journal of Family Issues*.

West, A., Roberts, J., Lewis, J. and Noden, P. (2015). Paying for higher education in England: Funding policy and families. *British Journal of Educational Studies*, 63(1): 23–45.

White, J. (2013). Thinking generations. *British Journal of Sociology*, 64(2): 216–247.

Willetts, D. (2010). *The Pinch: How the Baby Boomers Took Their Children's Future – and Why They Should Give It Back*. London: Atlantic Books.

Wintre, M. and Yaffe, M. (2000). First-year students' adjustment to university life as a function of relationship with parents. *Journal of Adolescent Research*, 15(1): 9–38.

1 Parents and students

Financial support and student independence

Introduction

As we have seen, there has been much debate in the UK about how young adults nowadays are more disadvantaged than their "baby boomer" parents. Indeed, the parents, as students, did not have to pay tuition fees and may also have received means-tested government grants to support their living costs. However, as a result of policies implemented over the past two decades by Conservative, Labour and Conservative-Liberal Democrat governments, the system of funding higher education and the provision of financial aid to students has undergone significant change. Students in our study were charged tuition fees, for which a loan was available for eligible students, and the main form of financial support for living costs was a means-tested loan.

In England, student mobility is 'embedded in the culture' of the higher education system (Holdsworth, 2009: 1,862) with the majority of students – around seven out of ten – choosing to live away from the family home while at university (UK House of Commons, 2013). The higher education funding system assumes that students are dependent on their families in that they are not eligible for financial support in their own right (unless certain conditions are fulfilled) (SLC, 2011), although the loan repayments are the responsibility of the graduate. As a result of the changes to the funding system, middle-class parents may give substantial material support to their children, thus extending their children's financial dependence (Ahier, 2000; Pollard et al., 2013).

We focus in this chapter on two main themes: on the one hand, the financial support parents provide for their student children and, on the other, students' views about their own financial independence. We first describe our overall approach before outlining the policy context. We then examine the extent and nature of parents' financial contributions to their student children, and associated tensions, before exploring students' perceptions of their financial independence. The final section discusses the findings and the relationship between parental financial support and students' views of their financial independence.

Our approach

Considerable attention has been devoted to exploring intergenerational transfer patterns in a range of European countries and the United States. Studies have tended to reveal similar results, namely that transfers between family members are frequent; that they tend to occur downward from older to younger generations; and that transfers from parents to adult children (or grandchildren) are often targeted at the most needy (Kohli, 2004). Thus, Fingerman et al. (2009) found that parents provide frequent support to grown children, with more being provided to some than to others, including those with serious health needs and those experiencing financial difficulties.

Specifically with respect to higher education, parental financial support of students has been explored in Europe (e.g., Antonucci, 2016) and extensively in the United States, where upper-middle-class parents regard contributions to the cost of college education as a parental obligation (Holmstrom et al., 2011). Middle-class parents frequently make difficult financial decisions regarding support; these can come at a considerable cost as parents 'dip into family savings or pull from retirement accounts' (Hamilton, 2013: 2). As financial support for students in the United Kingdom has, since its inception, been means-tested, some parents have been expected to contribute to their children's higher education costs although this does not necessarily mean that they do so (Hesketh, 1999). Moreover, if they do provide support it can cause difficulties for families. Finch and Mason (1993) describe the case of a student whose entitlement to a means-tested grant was not clear – because the assessment of his parents' income was complex – and in order to enable him to take up his place, the mother took up a factory job to pay for his university accommodation. Ahier (2000: 690) notes that families unable to invest intergenerationally may come 'under increasing stress, unable to fulfil the new obligations and expectations which simultaneous policy changes in education, pensions and welfare thrust upon them'. While the majority of students attending university are from middle-class backgrounds (see Introduction), there is heterogeneity within the middle classes which is likely to affect if and how parents financially support their children.

In England, students have traditionally moved away from home to study and the relationship between leaving home to go to university and gaining independence is 'so ubiquitous' that it is accepted by students and parents alike (Holdsworth, 2009: 1,858). Our interest in this chapter is in financial independence and what it means from the student's perspective, but as we shall see the notions were varied and could encompass what has been called autonomy – the ability to make decisions for oneself (Gaudet, 2001; see also Cicchelli, and Martin, 2004; Wintre and Yaffe, 2000). Quantitative research has found that there is a relationship between parental resources and students' reports of their financial independence. Thus, in one study students whose parents had higher incomes and assets were less likely to report that they felt financially independent than those with lower levels (Xiao et al., 2014). In another, a higher proportion of students who received lower levels of financial support reported perceiving themselves as an adult (Padilla-Walker et al., 2012). As qualitative research has revealed, independence is construed differently by young people and can incorporate notions of responsibility as an individual and of responsibility to others (Gillies et al., 2001); we might, therefore, expect financial independence to be understood differently.

Policy context

Turning to the policy context, it is important to stress that governments in different countries have adopted varying approaches to funding universities and supporting students' participation in higher education. Thus, in some countries no tuition fees are charged – for example, Sweden – while in others, such as England and the United States, tuition fee levels are high (OECD, 2016: 234). Approaches toward government financial aid for students also differ – in England students are seen as dependent on their parents, whereas in countries such as Sweden, they are seen as independent and not reliant on parents. Moreover, policy in some jurisdictions, including England, has changed dramatically in recent decades.[1]

Financial support for British students studying on full-time undergraduate degree programmes was introduced by the Conservative government in 1962. Students were able to apply for maintenance grants to help cover their living costs; these were means-tested and if the student was not awarded a full maintenance grant, parents were expected to make up the shortfall. From 1977, local education authorities paid tuition fees directly to higher education institutions (UK House of Commons, 1998). In the 1990s the Conservative government, under Margaret Thatcher, introduced significant policy changes to the funding of higher education. In particular, following legislation enacted in 1990, 'mortgage-style' student loans were introduced to provide additional resources towards students' living costs (see Barr, 2012).

During this period there was also a sharp increase in the proportion of young people entering higher education, with participation increasing from around 15 per cent to 30 per cent between 1987 and 1992 (Wilson, 1997). In

1996, the Conservative government set up a major enquiry into higher educa-tion – the National Committee of Inquiry into Higher Education (NCIHE). The ensuing report[2] (NCIHE, 1997) concluded that future higher education funding policy could not be reliant on increased public expenditure alone to meet the rising costs of higher education. The subsequent Labour government (1997–2010) accepted the Committee's recommendation that students – with the exception of those from the poorest families – should be charged univer-sity tuition fees (Department for Education and Employment, 1998). Follow-ing legislation enacted in 1998, virtually all new United Kingdom entrants to full-time higher education programmes were required to pay an upfront means-tested contribution towards tuition fees (this was originally £1,000).[3] Grants to assist with living costs were abolished – from 1999–2000 new full-time entrants to higher education received support for living costs by means of income-contingent loans alone (Student Loans Company, 2004). However, at this time there was no loan to cover the tuition fee.

Further changes followed the 2004 Higher Education Act, with "variable fees" of up to £3,000 per annum being introduced in 2006 for students on full-time undergraduate programmes at English higher education institu-tions.[4] The government justified the increase in tuition fees on grounds of the benefits that accrue to the individual: 'The benefits of higher education for individuals are far-reaching. On average, graduates get better jobs and earn more than those without higher education' (Department for Education and Skills, 2003: 4). Following the policy change, non-means-tested loans to cover tuition fees and means-tested loans to cover maintenance were intro-duced.[5] The graduate was required to start repaying the loan once she or he was earning above £15,000 a year; the loan attracted a zero real interest rate (Barr, 2012). The government also introduced a package of additional financial support for students from low-income backgrounds, namely the re-introduction of means-tested maintenance grants funded by government and mandatory university-funded cash bursaries (for students in receipt of the full maintenance grant). In addition, universities also offered discretionary bursa-ries to these students and others. The students who participated in our study commenced their studies in 2011–12, when tuition fees were up to £3,375 per annum.

There is an inextricable link between students and their families as regards the English higher education funding policy. At the time our study was car-ried out, students' access to higher levels of maintenance loans and grants was contingent on household income – if students were not in receipt of the maximum maintenance loan, the expectation was that parents/spouses would make up the difference. The main beneficiaries of parental financial support are likely to be middle-class students, the focus of our study. In 2011–12, almost 80 per cent of full-time students took out a tuition fee loan, and nearly 75 per cent took out a means-tested government maintenance loan; significantly, however, fewer students from managerial, professional or intermediate backgrounds than those from routine and manual work backgrounds took out such loans. The students who received the most parental help were from professional or managerial backgrounds (mean contribution around £2,300) and those who received the least were from manual backgrounds (mean around £700) (Pollard et al., 2013). Funding policy in England changed again in 2012–13 when tuition fees for new undergraduate students – not the students who participated in our study – increased further, up to £9,000 per annum, making them amongst the highest in the Organisation for Economic Co-operation and Development (OECD, 2016; see also Kirby, 2016).[6]

Our study

Of the 29 students in our sample (see Introduction), 28 were eligible for financial support from the UK government, and had at least one parent who had been to university; virtually all the parents had graduated from British universities and, as students, had received means-tested local authority maintenance grants. Our analysis focuses on parents' reports of financial arrangements except in those cases where students did not receive regular financial support from their parents. The issue of financial independence is addressed from the standpoint of the student.

A majority of parents (25 out of 29) provided their children with financial support; only four lone mothers on low incomes did not provide regular financial contributions. Parents also made other material contributions. The majority had paid for or contributed towards a laptop computer and in about half the cases they contributed to their children's mobile telephone costs by paying or sharing the costs of the monthly tariff. A wide range of other contributions were also mentioned including gym membership; clothes; train, bus and taxi fares; computer software and hardware; family holidays; haircuts; loans and occasional small cash gifts. The purchase of food for the student was frequently mentioned. Grandparents or other relatives supported over one in three students; they provided cash gifts and loans, supermarket vouchers, and assisted with accommodation costs.

In the following sections, we examine the extent and nature of parental financial contributions to their children's higher education studies, and in particular regular contributions to support living costs. We then examine students' perceptions of financial independence.

Higher education costs: parental contributions

The extent of the financial support provided to students by families varied and was related to household income which ranged from less than £25,000 a year to more than £58,000.[7] In a small number of cases (five), the family paid for all the student's higher education costs: tuition fees, accommodation and living expenses, with parental contributions ranging from an estimated £4,500 to £26,500 a year. In the majority of cases (20), parents made regular contributions to their students' living costs (£1,200 to £11,000 a year) supplementing government maintenance loans and in some cases grants. A small number of students (four) did not receive regular financial contributions from their parents but were in receipt of high levels of government financial support (loans and grants), and in some cases university bursaries on account of the low household income. All students except for those where all costs were paid by the family took out a government tuition fee loan (with fees being paid directly to the university).[8] In the sections below we examine the nature of parents' contributions to their children's higher education costs and in so doing explore associated tensions associated with the financial support provided.

Parents paid or considered paying all the costs

In five cases, the family paid all the costs for the children's higher education degree programme; in one of these families, the student and parents shared the costs. The principal reason given for paying all the costs was to avoid the child being in debt on graduation. As one mother commented: 'I don't want [my children] to end up with huge debts. . . . I'd rather sacrifice everything . . . and make sure that they don't . . . have . . . huge debts'. A different perspective was given by one father: 'We can afford to fund her. . . . I don't particularly like or trust having a government involved in any particular financial transaction'.

The processes by which parents offered support to their children were varied – in some cases the costs were shared between parents or between the parent and the student. So in one case the student's mother paid the tuition fees, and her father her living costs. The parents provided debit cards and the father monitored expenditure electronically: if their daughter spent money her account was topped up by her father. In another case, the parents contributed £4,500 and the student £2,000 per year from savings (including money he had earned and gifts). The student wanted to avoid taking out a loan – as he commented 'why get into debt if you can help it?' Nor did his father want him to take out a loan, noting that he had left university without any debt. This student lived on a mere £10 a week and was given food by his parents and supermarket vouchers by his grandmother.

Two parents had considered paying for all their children's higher education costs but decided that their children should take out the loan. In one case, the father – who was, in his words, 'very rich' – could have paid all the costs. While his daughter would 'pick up the loan', if there were any difficulties with regard to repayments he would be responsible – this would be a 'residual obligation'. The father paid his daughter's rent, but had not got round to working out 'exactly how much she needs': 'I give her £100 if she needs it. Usually when I'm there I give her some money as I leave. . . . You know we sort of muddle along'.

One mother could 'probably' have afforded to pay for her daughter's higher education costs, but did not want her daughter to be totally dependent; as the mother said: 'She needs to learn the value of money'. The mother described how she and her husband had divorced after he had inherited a large sum of money, and as part of the divorce settlement it had been agreed that he would provide for their daughter's university education; some of this money was being used to pay for the daughter's rent and the remainder could be used – perhaps – to pay off her student loans. The student's maintenance loan was paying for food and utilities; in addition, her mother provided 'lump sums' when needed, and an allowance earmarked for specific activities.

Regular parental financial contributions: constraints, tensions and conditions

In the majority of cases (20), parents made regular financial contributions to help with their children's living costs while at university. In a number of cases, parents wanted to contribute more than they did but could not because of their own financial situation. In particular, some parents were concerned about providing for their own retirement costs as well as supporting their student children. This meant that they had to make choices about how best to support their children while they were at university. In one case, the parents had already paid for their daughter's private education, but this had not been easy. They would have liked to have been able to pay all of her university costs, but as the mother noted the amount was 'quite huge': 'I felt that it was going to have an impact on us being able to provide for our pensions'. She did not feel that this was right so they had decided to pay their daughter's accommodation costs, with the daughter using her maintenance loan for the remaining living costs. The mother felt that the government loans were 'a bit like an extra tax, so it felt different': she would have been more averse to her children taking out a normal, commercial loan.

In another case the parents had paid for their daughter's living costs. However, the father commented that every pound they gave her was 'a pound less' for their retirement, and they had decided to allow their daughter to take out the maintenance loan. But in due course they would give her the money that they would have given her toward the tuition fees to help her buy a property. Similar tensions between financial support for children's higher education costs and retirement have been observed in the US where parental support for higher education amongst the upper middle classes is the norm, albeit that the systems of financial support are quite different (Holmstrom et al., 2011).

For other parents, there were different considerations. Some students had health-related needs and their parents decided to provide more support than they would otherwise have done. In one case, the mother paid the daughter's rent and the father gave her an allowance, but because of the daughter's health needs, the mother also agreed to the daughter using her maintenance loan to pay for a car, which she felt was 'a bit of an expensive luxury'. In another case, the parents paid for more expensive accommodation than they would otherwise have done, but in order to do so they had taken out a commercial loan. This they found 'really difficult' but they were willing to be 'a few thousand in debt' to enable their daughter to have the experience of going away to university. Being especially supportive of children with health problems chimes with the findings of Fingerman et al. (2009), namely that parents provided more support to children with particular needs. Research carried out in the US has also found that parents may take out commercial loans to support their children's higher education costs (e.g., Holmstrom et al., 2011).

The way in which the English financial support system worked caused significant stress for some parents. In part this is because loans are means-tested and also because even the full amount of the loan was insufficient to meet typical board and lodging costs.[9] One mother assumed that the government financial aid would be enough for her daughter to live on and was 'absolutely shocked looking at the maths' that this 'only paid . . . the rent and she couldn't eat'. She was not at the time working but decided that she needed to find a job (cf. Finch and Mason, 1993). As a result, she was able to give her daughter a monthly allowance. Another mother was also 'a bit shocked at the money side of things'. Financial issues were problematic as two of her children would be at university alongside each other. She had already given her son money to help him pay off a 'large chunk' of his student debt – she 'put it aside years ago in the hope that it would pay student fees. Now things have got much harder for students . . . it might pay half of it, it might not pay that much'. For this family, there was an aim that both children should come out of university with similar levels of debt. Even though they had planned for their children's university costs, they had not anticipated the substantial increase in tuition fees to £9,000 per year from 2012–13, which would affect their second child.

The obligations of parents both to support their children financially and to be equitable were elaborated by another mother. She and her husband paid their daughter's rent and the daughter had taken out a student loan.

However, the mother had encouraged her to get a part-time job in order to save some of her loan. As a result, her daughter had not really had 'to touch any of the maintenance loan money'. The government loan – which had relatively favourable repayment terms[10] – had been invested in a savings account, and the plan was that it could be used to pay off part of the loan in one lump sum in due course. Had the parents known when their children were younger that they would have to pay for their university education (albeit that they were not obliged to do so), they could have started saving when their children were babies. Moreover, if their son were to go to university, they felt that they would have to do the same for him as they had done for their daughter. Both parents disliked debt and were worried that their children would begin their adult lives 'with this debt'.

Although parents' accounts revealed that they felt obligations to support their children, this was not invariably the case. Thus, in one case, the student was not awarded a government grant as her father's income was too high, and while the father (who was estranged from the mother) should have topped up her loan – as intended by government policy – he did not provide the full amount, creating financial difficulties for the student. Her situation was exacerbated as she was providing financial support to her unemployed mother.

In some cases, parental financial support was dependent on the student child behaving in what the parents considered to be a responsible way. The conditionality was of various types and could relate to study or to paid work. The parents of one student wanted their daughter to view her degree 'like a full-time job'; according to the father:

> I said, "I don't mind if you go and get a little part-time job, but I don't want the thought of you working 20, 25 hours a week in a supermarket or something at the cost of your degree, 'cause you are, effectively, paying for that and it would be a shame, so we'll give you enough to live on".

In another case, the parents expected their daughter to undertake paid work. They had a 'good income' and as the maintenance loan did not cover the rent, they were giving her a monthly allowance. However, they had decided that the daughter would have to take a part-time job because this was the 'responsible thing to do and you . . . can't expect everybody to just hand it all to you'. In yet another case, there were different conditions: the student's mother commented that the allowance was not to be used to finance 'a load of boozing'. These varying ideas are consistent with the description by Holmstrom et al. (2011: 282) of parents who believe that their children had a responsibility to focus on their studies: 'to work hard in college, to learn . . . to "take it seriously" . . . and not to be "party-mad"'.

Minimal parental financial support and high levels of government financial aid

Four students who lived with lone mothers received no regular financial assistance from their parents. They received both a government maintenance loan and a grant; two also received a university bursary. While there was minimal parental financial support in all four cases – for example, train fares, food purchases, help with mobile telephone bills, small cash payments – two students received support from other relatives.

One student was able to ask her elderly grandmother for help: 'She's 86 and living on her own so she doesn't spend her money on anything and she always says that she'd rather us have it now than when she's dead'. The grandmother had also paid for the student's brother to undertake a master's degree. However, the support was conditional as her grandmother would not 'give money for like stupid things, but when it comes to things like education, housing and rent then she's very happy to help and pay which is really good'. Another student, whose parents were divorced and who had no contact with his father, lived in the house of a relative rent free.

Two students whose parents were also divorced reported that their fathers had saved money for them – either paying money into a building society savings account or taking out life insurance policies. However, one of the students had, in turn, given her mother several hundred pounds: 'I've been sending money over to my mum via bank transfer because she doesn't have an income at present'.

Financial independence

As we have seen, the financial arrangements for meeting the higher education costs of the student children varied: the family paid all of the children's higher education costs in five cases; 20 students took out government tuition fee loans and maintenance loans (or loans and grants) to help cover their living costs and also received regular financial contributions from their parents to supplement the government financial support; and four students from low-income, lone-parent families received grants, loans and in some cases university bursaries, but no regular financial support from their parents.

Where families paid all the costs, no students reported working during term-time and none reported borrowing money via a bank overdraft. One student said that although not financially independent, she was 'able to make the decisions independently'; this was not something she had done before. Parents also supported their children with their financial planning. As one student noted: 'We did a budget before I came to uni . . . what I should spend on each week like £20 on food' and she was, in addition, given advice: 'My dad said I should never go in to overdraft'.

Amongst the 20 students where parents made regular financial contributions, 11 worked during term-time – for example in retail work; in a call centre; doing care work; doing administrative work on the campus; selling paintings; and from music. Three were using their own savings to support themselves and five students used a bank overdraft. One commented that her father had recently helped her out because she 'literally had no money left'. She had considered getting an overdraft, but her father did not want her to do so: 'He thinks they're really . . . risky'. These students varied in terms of their perceptions of financial independence; their understandings related to control over their budgets and managing their money. For one, parental financial support had helped her become more independent as her parents gave her a 'lump sum' and it was her responsibility to decide how to spend it so 'you do . . . learn how to manage your finances'. Another student felt financially 'quite independent' in that she could manage her day-to-day money, albeit that her father managed her savings on her behalf.

Several students felt that they should not have to rely on parental financial support. One in receipt of high levels of government support, who received a small monthly allowance from her father, stressed not 'feeling' like a child (cf. Mary, 2014):

> I'm 20 now. . . . I just feel like I'm not their child anymore. They don't have to pay for things for me. . . . In the government's eyes I think they shouldn't be paying for things for me.

In their accounts, students made reference to the importance of earning money and independence. One felt 'quite bad . . . it doesn't really seem fair. . . . I don't like taking money from my parents'. She had worked when she was at school so she could buy her computer and 'quite liked having independence money wise'. Another had also worked during her first year. She was happy about this, as it meant that she could go travelling without having to ask her parents for money: 'I don't feel I should do that. . . . I want to be kind of independent and not rely on them'. Earning money also meant that she was able to lend her parents some money for a few days when they were a 'little overdrawn'. Learning how to manage finances was at the forefront of this student's mind as the following year she was to live in a flat which was 'going to be even more of . . . a learning curve' for her 'in terms of being more thrifty'.

Although students who received regular financial support from their parents alongside government financial aid could feel independent, some parents wanted to retain a degree of control over their children's finances. One student reported that her father had offered her a financial incentive if she provided details of her expenditure. She did this for a while, but then decided that she would rather not have him 'intervene in my financial matters, because I don't want him to know what I'm spending my money on'. In this case, the desire to control how she spent her money led the student to forgo the additional money on offer from her father. In a similar vein, another student had changed his bank account and address so that his statements could not be opened by his father. Others were also striving for more autonomy even though they were financially dependent. A student and his sister, who was also at university, had explicitly and overtly negotiated[11] with their father about how he should provide financial support. The father had suggested that he should pay for their living expenses. However, they had persuaded him to pay for their university student hall fees instead; this gave them more control about how they spent their maintenance loans.

Four students were in receipt of higher levels of state support – loans and grants – and received no regular parental contributions; two had worked occasionally in term-time, both in catering; and two had been overdrawn, one by £1,000. These students tended to have strong views about their financial arrangements. Two were explicit about being financially independent. One said she had become 'entirely' independent. Her parents were not involved with her financial arrangements and she did not talk to them about money; she had set her own budget 'from the start' and wanted to 'take control of it'. This gave her autonomy as she was spending money on 'things like alcohol'. She did not feel that it would be justifiable to take money from her parents when it was not all spent on the 'best things in the world'.

A student, who felt almost 'completely independent', emphasised the significance of state financial support: he felt that there 'was no other possible way that I could . . . fund my education . . . there's absolutely no way that my mum could afford to pay towards my halls [accommodation] and my loan'. He commented that if she did financially support him 'to a great extent', then he would feel more dependent on his mother.

The importance of privacy and financial control were also raised. One student reported that her (now deceased) father had looked at her older brothers' bank accounts and how they spent their money when they were at university. She did not have 'any of that control which is probably a good thing 'cos some of the things I spend my money on, like clothes, he wouldn't be very happy about'. In a similar vein, another student sought control of his finances – and privacy – from his mother, but acknowledged that he was learning how to manage his finances:

[S]he'll . . . say "how are you doing with your money" and then I'll . . . fend her off . . . I'll be like "yeah, it's all right". . . . I like to think I can budget independently, I know I can't, but I like to think I can. . . . I think eventually I will get the hang of it, well I'm going to have to, it's just . . . a learning curve at the moment, I guess.

Discussion and conclusion

The vast majority of the predominantly middle-class parents in our sample with children at long-established universities made regular financial contributions to their student children. There was, however, much variation within the sample, associated with varying levels of household affluence. In a small proportion of cases, families paid all the costs – tuition fees and living costs – but in the main, parents gave regular contributions, supplementing government loans for living costs (students took out the government tuition fee loan to cover fees levied by universities). However, this could be stressful for parents and result in tensions regarding the need to save for their pensions and to contribute towards their student children's higher education costs. Some parents provided only limited financial support, in the main because they could not afford to contribute, but on occasion because they were unwilling to do so. Other intergenerational transfers were common, with relatives, especially grandparents, contributing towards higher education costs – for example, providing cash or supermarket vouchers.

In terms of actual contributions, parents contributed to differing extents and some were able to protect their children from debt. More affluent parents paid the higher education costs in whole or in part; some put money aside for future property purchases – crucially important for young adults to attain independent housing in the UK (Heath, 2017); and others encouraged their children to save the government maintenance loan, given its favourable – at that time – repayment terms. In this way, wealthier parents were able to transmit their financial advantage to their children, thus exacerbating intragenerational inequality. Christie and Munro (2003: 633) reported that 'parents play a much greater role in supporting their student sons and daughters than is generally recognised'. While the policy assumption is that the debt is the responsibility of the graduate, this is clearly not the case for some families where debt is a family affair.

Although most students benefited from financial support from their parents, some did not (see also Hesketh, 1999). In these cases, students could be left in precarious positions, as money assumed by the government to be paid to students by parents (to supplement the means-tested loan) was not provided. Some students were thus in situations that were financially stressful. This could also be exacerbated when they supported parents financially. In short, while students from low-income households were in receipt of more money from the state and in some cases from the university, they were clearly at a disadvantage compared with those from better off families where additional familial resources were available.

Students' perceptions of their financial independence were associated with levels of parental financial support. Some had learned to manage their finances and to become more responsible about how they spent money. This can be seen to be related to the idea of "learning independence" (cf. Gillies et al., 2001). These notions of independence – to do with making decisions for oneself – can also be understood as "autonomy" (Gaudet, 2001). The students' accounts also acknowledged that there was a "learning curve" associated with financial autonomy, as in the case of budgeting with parental support, and learning how to be thrifty. An important element of financial independence for some students was earning money.

Some students wanted privacy in their financial affairs; this is a key element of financial autonomy (Bennett and Sung, 2013). A desire for privacy has also been identified in other situations, with students wishing certain aspects of their private lives to be kept away from their parents (West et al., 2009). Students are at a transition point and may seek to distance themselves from their parents. Holdsworth (2009: 1,858) notes that the notion of independence epitomised by students is 'freedom to be oneself' without interference from parents. Some students' accounts of financial arrangements clearly reinforce this view.

Another dimension of independence is taking responsibility for others (Gillies et al., 2001); this is clearly demonstrated in the case of the students who provided financial support for their unemployed mothers.

Students whose parents did not provide any regular financial support and who received maintenance loans and grants reported that they felt financially independent of their families. These students had autonomy over how they used their money and they also took responsibility for their own financial budgeting. The findings suggest a relationship between parental financial support and students' views about financial independence. In short, low levels of parental financial support and high levels of government support were associated with feelings of independence. One student commented:

> some of my friends are more dependent on their parents . . . because their student loan doesn't cover everything 'cos they're . . . wealthier their parents need to cover it, they have . . . a stronger financial dependency.

In conclusion, only a minority of students – those in receipt of high levels of government financial support with no regular contributions from their parents – felt that they were financially independent. Others could feel independent as regards the management of their money. For some, earning money was important as regards feelings of independence (see also Chapter 4). Parents, for their part, could help their children learn to become more financially independent, although some also sought to exert a measure of control over their children's finances and impose conditions in order to encourage what they felt to be responsible behaviour.

Notes

1 See Callender (2014) for an informative account of how ideas regarding tuition fees, grants and loans have changed over the past 50 years.
2 Commonly referred to as the Dearing Report (the Committee was chaired by Ron Dearing).
3 The amount depended on their own, their parents' or their spouse's income.
4 See Minty (2015) for an overview of policy changes in Scotland.
5 This is in contrast to the US where much student debt is held by private lenders, which tend to have strict conditions regarding repayment. Federal loans are not all income-contingent (Kirby, 2016).
6 Under the new funding arrangements, from 2016, graduates begin to make loan repayments when their income reaches £21,000 with a real (above-inflation) interest rate up to 3 per cent (Crawford and Jin, 2014).
7 This was derived from the information provided on the level of student loans and grants and relates only to the 28 students eligible for UK government financial support (see West et al., 2015).
8 See West et al. (2015) for more details of financial arrangements for students eligible for UK government financial support at the time the study was carried out.
9 Based on information provided by a sample of universities, the government loan and assessed parental contribution was lower than the amount needed to live away from home, estimated to be approximately £8,000–£9,000 per academic year for 2011–12.
10 Under the funding regime introduced in 2012–13, the loan terms are no longer as favourable (see Concluding reflections).
11 See Finch and Mason (1993) for a discussion of different types of negotiations.

References

Ahier, J. (2000). Financing higher education by loans and fees: Theorizing and researching the private effects of a public policy. *Journal of Education Policy*, 15(6): 683–700.
Antonucci, L. (2016). *Student Lives in Crisis: Deepening Inequality in Times of Austerity*. Bristol: Policy Press.
Barr, N. (2012). The higher education white paper: The good, the bad, the unspeakable – and the next white paper. *Social Policy and Administration*, 46(5): 483–508.

Bennett, F. and Sung, S. (2013). Dimensions of financial autonomy in low-/moder ate-income couples from a gender perspective and implications for welfare reform. *Journal of Social Policy*, 42(4): 701–719.

Callender, C. (2014). Student Numbers and Funding: Does Robbins Add Up? *Higher Education Quarterly*, 68(2): 164–186.

Christie, H. and Munro, M. (2003). The logic of loans: Students' perceptions of the costs and benefits of the student loan. *British Journal of Sociology of Education*, 24(5): 621–636.

Cicchelli, V. and Martin, C. (2004). Young adults in France: Becoming adult in the context of increased autonomy and dependency. *Journal of Comparative Family Studies*, 35(4): 615–626.

Crawford, C. and Jin, W. (2014). *Payback Time? Student Debt and Loan Repayments: What Will the 2012 Reforms Mean for Graduates?* London: IFS.

Department for Education and Employment (DfEE). (1998). *The Government's Response to Higher Education in the Learning Society: The Report of the National Committee of Inquiry Into Higher Education*. London: DfEE.

Department for Education and Skills. (2003). *The Future of Higher Education, Cm 5735*. London: The Stationery Office.

Finch, J. and Mason, J. (1993). *Negotiating Family Responsibilities*. London: Routledge.

Fingerman, K., Miller, L., Birditt, K. and Zarit, S. (2009). Giving to the good and needy: Parental support of grown children. *Journal of Marriage and Family*, 71: 1220–1233.

Gaudet, S. (2001). La responsabilité dans les débuts de l'âge adulte. *Lien social et Politiques*, 46(2): 71–83.

Gillies, V., Ribbens McCarthy, J. and Holland, J. (2001). *'Pulling Together, Pulling Apart': The Family Lives of Young People*. London: Family Policy Studies Centre for Joseph Rowntree Foundation.

Hamilton, L. T. (2013). More is more or more Is less? Parental financial investments during college. *American Sociological Review*, 78(1): 70–95.

Heath, S. (2017). Siblings, fairness and parental support for housing in the UK. *Housing Studies*. doi: 10.1080/02673037.2017.1291914

Hesketh, A. (1999). Towards an economic sociology of the student financial experience of higher education. *Journal of Education Policy*, 14(4): 385–410.

Holdsworth, C. (2009). "Going away to uni": Mobility, modernity, and independence of English higher education students. *Environment and Planning A*, 41: 1850–1864.

Holmstrom, L. L., Karp, V. and Gray, P. S. (2011). Why parents pay for college: The good parent, perceptions of advantage, and the intergenerational transfer of opportunity. *Symbolic Interaction*, 34(2): 265–289.

Kirby, P. (2016). *Degrees of Debt: Funding and Finance for Undergraduates in Anglophone Countries*. London: Sutton Trust.

Kohli, M. (2004). Intergenerational transfers and inheritance: A comparative view. *Annual Review of Gerontology and Geriatrics*, 24(1): 266–289.

Mary, A. A. (2014). Re-evaluating the concept of adulthood and the framework of transition. *Journal of Youth Studies*, 17(3): 415–429.

Minty, S. (2015). Young people's attitudes towards student debt in Scotland and England. In S. Ridell, E. Weedon and S. Minty (Eds.), *Higher Education in Scotland and the UK: Diverging or Converging Systems?* (pp. 56–70). Edinburgh: Edinburgh University Press.

National Committee of Inquiry into Higher Education (NCIHE). (1997). *Higher Education in the Learning Society*. London: HMSO.

OECD. (2016). *Education at a Glance 2016*. Paris: OECD.

Padilla-Walker, L. M., Nelson, L. J. and Carroll, J. S. (2012). Affording emerging adulthood: Parental financial assistance of their college-aged children. *Journal of Adult Development*, 19(1): 50–58.

Pollard, E., Hunt, W., Hillage, J., Drever, E., Chanfreau, J., Coutinho, S. and Poole, E. (2013). *Student Income and Expenditure Survey 2011/12: English-Domiciled Students*. London: Department for Business, Innovation and Skills.

Student Loans Company (SLC). (2004). *Statistics of Student Support for Higher Education in the United Kingdom – Financial Year 2003–2004 and Academic Year 2004–2005 (Provisional)*. Glasgow: SLC.

Student Loans Company (SLC). (2011). *Higher Education Student Finance – How You Are Assessed and Paid 2011/12*. Glasgow: SLC.

UK House of Commons. (1998). *The teaching and higher education bill [HL]: Financial provision for higher and further education*. Research Paper 98/33. London: House of Commons Library.

UK House of Commons. (2013, October 15). Written Answers, Hansard Vol. 568 col 684–685W.

West, A., Lewis, J. and Currie, P. (2009). Students' Facebook 'friends': Public and private spheres. *Journal of Youth Studies*, 12(6): 615–627.

West, A., Roberts, J., Lewis, J. and Noden, P. (2015). Paying for higher education in England: Funding policy and families. *British Journal of Educational Studies*, 63(1): 23–45.

Wilson, W. (1997). *Student grants, loans and tuition fees*. Research Paper Number 97/119. London: House of Commons Library.

Wintre, M. and Yaffe, M. (2000). First-year students' adjustment to university life as a function of relationship with parents. *Journal of Adolescent Research*, 15(1): 9–38.

Xiao, J. J., Chatterjee, S. and Kim, J. (2014). Factors associated with financial independence of young adults. *International Journal of Consumer Studies*, 38: 394–403.

2 Students and parents

Communication, emotional and practical support, and independence

Introduction

Studies in the UK and US have shown an increased level of contact between parents and millennial students. Indeed, the majority of the parents interviewed for this study reported that they had had relatively little contact with their own parents when at university. The media and academic studies have documented the changes in the nature and extent of contact between this generation and their student children, with the idea of "overparenting", or "helicopter parenting" a major issue. However, as Schiffrin et al. (2014) have shown, greater contact and involvement may mean different things: parental encouragement, for example, for the student to deal with his or her own relationship or practical problems; parental monitoring of matters such as diet or friends; or direct parental intervention, such as how often to telephone home, or, at the extreme, involving direct contact with the university authorities with or without the student's knowledge. Some of these behaviours are likely to encourage more autonomy on the part of the student, some are not.

Indeed, the debate has focused on whether greater parental involvement retards the progress that students might make towards more autonomous thinking and action, and greater independence (see Introduction). Our analysis focuses on the *kind* of interaction that takes place between parents and students in the context of the often strident debate about "helicopter parents" (Coburn, 2006; Padilla-Walker and Nelson, 2012) and delayed adulthood. However, while a few of the parents in our sample described behaviours that could be characterised as overprotective or overly intense, and while some of the students also showed that they continued to depend on their parents for help and advice ranging from recipes to the treatment of coughs and colds and the operation of a bank account, almost all showed awareness of the importance of what most referred to as "independence". Chapter 1 showed that the financial situation of the students varied, but the majority were supported by their parents financially. In this chapter, we also find that the vast majority are in close or very close contact with their parents and receive considerable emotional and practical help. However, there is no discernible relationship between financial arrangements and non-financial support.

This chapter focuses on the support sought by and given to the students in our sample. It begins with an outline of our overall approach and then addresses the *frequency and nature* of the interaction between parents and students: who contacts whom and by what means, as well as how often. The main part of the analysis looks at the *reasons for contact* on the part of the students – emotional support, help with academic work, help with everyday tasks, and filial duty or simple regard for the parent – and also comments on the parents' reactions and reasons for taking the initiative in making contact. The chapter then considers the students' ideas about the importance (or otherwise) of the parental home, and the views of both students and parents about the possibility of the students returning to it, thus providing a bridge to Chapters 3 and 4. Finally, we discuss the degree of "independence" the students feel they have achieved, and whether this accords with the views of their parents.

Our approach

The greater freedom and independence associated with living away from home is part of what is now usually referred to as the "university experience" for English university students, albeit an experience that, as Holdsworth (2009) observes, has been largely an élite practice. Living away from home, usually only during the university terms, may well provide greater freedom, but is unlikely to result in full independence in the sense of self-reliance and the capacity to care for oneself (Ryan and Lynch, 1989; Whittington and Peters, 1996). The allied concept of autonomy, defined in terms of self-governance and taking responsibility for self, alongside a degree of separation from parents and the family home (Wintre and Yaffe, 2000; see also Gaudet, 2001; Gillies et al., 2001), is probably a more realistic representation of what students might expect to achieve. Furthermore, Ryan and Lynch (1989) have observed that if parents insist on independence rather than providing a supportive relationship for the encouragement of autonomy, separation may come at the expense of a secure parent-child relationship (see also Soenens et al., 2007).

Traditionally, the achievement of adulthood has been identified by social structural measures: living independently of the parental home, getting a job, marrying and having children (Furstenberg et al., 2004). However, Arnett (2000), a psychologist, identified "emerging adulthood" as a new developmental category, defined by taking responsibility for self and making independent decisions. In a sample of 346 US college students, he found that the most important criteria for making the transition to adulthood were: accepting responsibility for own actions, deciding on beliefs and values independently of parents, and establishing a relationship with parents as an equal adult (Arnett, 1994). Given the "halfway house" of living away from home at university, we would not expect to find students achieving this degree of independence. Indeed, Chapters 3 and 4 – on graduates returning to the parental home – show that it can remain difficult to achieve for some time after university. For while, as Newman (2012: 35) has commented, a 'psychological theory' of adulthood has become pervasive, structural obstacles to achieving adult independence (particularly a lack of jobs and housing) provide the context for individual decisions (Côté and Bynner, 2008). It seems likely that both sociological and psychological perspectives are important, as Pillemer et al. (2007: 777) have suggested, intergenerational relationships 'revolve around sociological and psychological *contradictions and dilemmas*' (their ital.).

But does contact with and support from parents hinder the move towards autonomy and independence, as many of the press articles and some of the psychological studies of "helicopter parenting" have suggested? Needless to say, the answer in much of the literature is that "it depends". Drawing on attachment theory, some have argued that a secure base in the form of parents and the parental home aids rather than threatens the development of autonomy (Kenny et al., 1987; Wartman and Savage, 2008). Kenny (1987: 26) found that first-year college students at a prestigious US university welcomed their parents' involvement, perceiving them 'as supporting independence and as being available as a source of support when needed' (see also Cullaty, 2011; Fingerman et al., 2012; Koepke and Denissen, 2012). However, the idea of "helicopter parenting" carries with it the notion of intensive interaction between parent and child, which may also be controlling (Padilla-Walker and Nelson, 2012); parents may be more or less committed to "letting go" of their children (Kloep and Hendry, 2010). On balance, psychologists have endorsed parental involvement with their young adult children as long as they value the goal of achieving independence and social competence (Schultheiss and Blustein, 1994; Sorokou and Weissbrod, 2005; Wartman et al., 2008). Indeed, the achievement of greater autonomy by the student may be more difficult when either the student or the parent is "emotionally detached" (Koepke and Denissen, 2012).

The American sociological literature published towards the end of the twentieth century sought particularly to stress the importance of family solidarity in face of the fears expressed by the political Right and some academics about family change and the decline of the traditional family (e.g.,

Bellah et al., 1985; Bengtson et al., 2002). But neither family solidarity nor conflict adequately captures the nature of and reasons for parent-student child interaction. Indeed, both parents and students may feel ambivalent about how much contact to make and support to seek or give. Cicchelli and Martin (2004) have remarked on the fact that young adults can affirm autonomy and dependence at the same time, while Gillies et al. (2001) have suggested that it is possible to be autonomous and also interdependent (see also Scabini et al., 2006; Settersten, 2012). Karp et al. (2004: 358–359, 374) have described the balance that many parents seek in their relationships with their young adult children in terms of 'distance and engagement', and a process of encouraging the young person to have both 'roots' and 'wings'. This found considerable support in some of the accounts of our parent respondents who talked about the difficulty of achieving a "balance", and whose feelings about their involvement with their student children were sometimes ambivalent. On the whole, the students expressed greater contentment with their situation, and were often able to feel that they could act autonomously even though they depended so much on parental support.

For this chapter we have focused on 27 of the 29 parents and student children we interviewed (see Introduction for details). We excluded two sets of parents and students in which the students offered more support to their mothers than *vice versa*, largely because of illness.

Maintaining contact

Frequency

Contact between parents and their student children has increased over time; Wartman and Savage (2008: 1) refer to a 'new level of family involvement'. Indeed, the kind of non-financial support we are talking about in this chapter tends to require regular contact, usually via mobile phones or computers, and also visits. However, when the parent respondents for this study were students, a public, pay telephone or letter writing were usually the only modes of day-to-day communication. One mother reported that her mother used to forward her mail with 'are you dead or just having fun?' written on the outside because she telephoned so rarely.

It is difficult to provide an accurate report on the frequency of communication between student and parent. First, even in intact families the parent interviewed often had little idea as to how often the student contacted the other parent. Second, reports on both frequency and even more on who initiated contact often differed between parents and students. Finally, both frequency and initiation of contact varied over time. In particular, contact increased markedly at a time of student crisis (see also Fingerman et al.,

2009). Two-thirds of students had crises during their first year; the first term and examination period were often difficult. Crises often concerned social relationships, but were also about academic work and practical problems, for example, regarding stolen goods. While the student usually initiated contact at a time of crisis, anxiety on the part of the parent about the student's welfare and safety often contributed to more frequent communication for a considerable period of time.

The most important mode of contact was by telephone call and by text (see also Stein et al., 2016). Telephone calls were usually reserved for more serious conversations and could be long or short (a male student said that the telephone created a 'more formal tone'). Texts were more often used by students and fathers to "keep in touch", or by some parents "just to check". Four sets of students and parents had tried Skype 'a couple of times', but in most cases, visits were frequent enough to make this kind of communication, which required greater organisation, unnecessary. Facebook and email were used by a minority and there was sometimes a reluctance on the part of some students to allow parents to be Facebook "friends"; in two cases, parents persisted until this became possible.[1] Facebook contact was common with siblings.

A majority of our sample of parents and children were in what might be regarded as frequent contact. Sarigiani et al. (2013) defined frequent as daily, or two or more times per day, while Spence (2012) drew a dividing line between those in contact once a week or less, and those in contact more than once a week. About a third of the students and parents were in contact on a weekly basis, another third multiple times a week, and a final third were in contact daily (see also Stein et al., 2016). In the case of students getting in touch weekly, most were male. The two South Asian students were in close contact; the male telephoned once a week and also went home every weekend. No parent and student were in touch on a less than weekly basis. In addition, most students visited home about twice a term and most parents also visited their child at university once or twice a term. All the students except one returned home in the vacation periods. A male student, who was in contact with his parents every day, said: 'I . . . thought it's like giving up if I go home. . . . I wanted to like stick it out and prove that I was capable of handling myself'. Visits home were much more common at times of emotional and academic crisis and for periods of examination revision: 'It's so much more chilled at home, most of the time . . . you . . . can breathe a bit' (female student).

Who makes contact

Parents often initiated contact with their offspring, even when – as in the case of two fathers – they said that they wanted them to be as independent as possible. Mothers tended to contact their daughters as much or more than *vice versa*. Both mothers and fathers said that they would initiate contact when the student had failed to do so, although one mother said that she texted so as not to 'interfere' if she had not heard from her daughter for two days. Some students reported contacting both parents (including absent parents), sometimes for different purposes. Thus one daughter relied more on her father for reassurance about her academic work while a son had depended hugely on his mother to talk him through his first-year crisis (contact with his father remained at the level of chat).

Mothers and daughters dominated our sample and the reports of who contacted whom often varied. In several cases the mother said that her daughter tended to initiate contact, but the daughters claimed it was '50/50'. One of these mothers said that her daughter called five times a day, but the daughter claimed: 'I mean my mum rings a lot and it's like, "Oh I'll ring you back later", but then sometimes I'll ring her and she's like "Oh can you ring later, I'm busy" . . . so . . . we're quite relaxed about that'. A second mother said that she did not always respond to her daughter, which made the daughter cross: ' "But I sent you something" ', to which the mother said she would respond: ' "Well . . . I've been busy" '. A third mother seemed to want her daughter (who admitted to being very dependent) to become much more autonomous, but also said: 'I mean, I'm very close to my children so we talk every day'. This raises the issue of how far the parent's behaviour actually matched what they wanted their children to achieve in terms of independence in particular.

Intergenerational changes in patterns of contact

Most of the parents in the sample agreed that *their* parents had wanted above all to know that they were 'all right'; as one put it: 'It wasn't for emotional support, parents didn't do that'. Many were quick to attribute the changes in their own patterns of communication with their student children to 'new technology', especially the mobile telephone, but also stressed that they wanted to be closer to their children and maintain closer relationships than had been the case with their own parents.

However, several parents expressed concern that their children should not feel 'any sense of obligation or duty' to get in touch, as one father put it. This father went on to say 'I didn't want her [his daughter] to feel that being away from home was a problem for us'. Parents who recognised that they had called home out of loyalty or duty alone did not want their children to do the same. One lone mother said that she did not want her son to 'feel that he needs to ring me . . . at a particular time, particular day'. It transpired that this had been expected of her and that she had telephoned her parents once a week. A few parents explicitly referred to what one referred to as the 'risk of over-parenting . . . certainly middle-class parents are very precious about their children aren't they? . . . sometimes you can overdo it and end up with neurotic children, can't you?'. This mother felt that it was important to listen, but she did not wish to direct her daughter in any way. Nevertheless, mother and daughter were in contact three or four times a week and the mother would call after a couple of days if she had not heard from her daughter. Indeed, parent and student lives were often closely intertwined. One student said that she had little to tell her parents when they did meet face-to-face; they knew it all already.

The reasons students contact parents

There were three main reasons for students to get in touch with their parents: the need for emotional support, for day-to-day practical advice and for support with academic work. However, it is also important to consider the relatively small number of students who maintained regular contact with their parents to some extent out of duty, loyalty, or because they thought that their parents might miss them and be lonely.

Emotional support

Contact was mainly about the provision of emotional support which involved the student talking over problems and anxieties and the parent offering reassurance. One father said that 'young people, when they leave home, they like to know that . . . they can show their concerns, which is nice actually because it implies that . . . there are good relations with us'.

Two female students lived in student accommodation but went home each Sunday for lunch. The mother of one of these said that she offered 'no sort of prescriptive emotional support', but that these visits allowed her daughter to 'manage the transition'. Most parents mentioned the importance of responding to the needs of their offspring, for example acting as a 'sounding board', which inferred an awareness of the importance of 'standing back' and actively seeking a new balance in the relationship. However, a small minority of parents continued to press for a much greater involvement in their children's lives. For example, a mother who maintained close contact with her daughter and who did not hesitate to take the initiative both in contacting her and the university authorities or the daughter's landlord (behaviour often categorised as "intensive" or "helicopter parenting") said: 'I think a lot of it [her interventions] is how I am . . . I like things to be right and . . . I wouldn't like her to not have the best life she can'. The South Asian parents also tended to remain deeply involved in the day-to-day lives of their children. As one mother put it: 'Is she eating bad . . . what's she eating and did she get up on time, how is she managing everything . . . I think of her all the time'.

The vast majority of students welcomed frequent contact with their parents. Some just wanted to keep in touch, but more common was the idea of the parent as a 'listening ear' or a safety net. One student who felt that she was 'allowed to be emotionally independent' also felt that her mother provided her with 'back-up', while a mother said that having urged her son to go to university, she felt a responsibility to help him.

Several students who contacted their parents when they experienced a crisis in their first term, often because of difficult social situations, usually wanted to go home. But even parents who were very involved in their student children's lives tended to respond negatively. One mother said that her daughter wanted her parents to say ' "Ooh, when are you coming home?" . . ., but we didn't think that was the right way to go'. Another mother also told her daughter not to 'pack it in, just stay with it. You know, this is quite normal, really. Just stay the course', even though she said that she wanted to jump in the car and fetch her. Interestingly it was a father who rushed home when his daughter telephoned in tears only a few days after arriving at university to say that she was coming home: 'I literally had to sort of ring up, cancel the business meeting, cross platforms, jump on the train straight back to . . . see her'.

A student acknowledged that she did not want to hear her parents' view that she should 'stick it out': 'I guess I wanted them to be like: "That's fine. Just come home and you can doss about and it's going to be really easy and we'll solve all your problems for you" '. She continued to seek help frequently with practical day-to-day problems. Some of these students were among those who also felt that they had to return home during the examination period, for reassurance, but also for the 'comforts' of home. Two confessed that they tended to be 'drama queens'. All these students were female, but male students also sought reassurance when facing difficulties, although they did not report reacting to crises in quite the same way, seeing their parents more in terms of a 'source of stability and a safety net'.

Day-to-day practical advice

Six students faced crises over more day-to-day matters, typically involving the theft of a bank card, bag, passport or laptop. All their parents offered advice, but varied in terms of how far they played a part in resolving the problem. The mother who said that her daughter called her all the time nevertheless reported that she 'was on the phone for three days sorting it [a stolen bag] out'. However, it was rather more common for parents to explain to the student how to go about solving the problem for themselves.

Nevertheless, many students sought help with quite small and simple matters, for example, how to prepare a leek and how long a cheque takes to clear. As a mother explained, 'she didn't understand the concept of . . . you've paid for something today and it hasn't gone through your account yet'. The South Asian parents in the sample expected to advise their children on everyday tasks and also provided food for them to take back to university when they returned home.

At the other end of the spectrum, a very few parents wanted to provide more support than the students were prepared to accept. A father said about his son:

> I actually feel I would like to give more support than he's asking for . . . there's an element of: "Hey I'm still your parent, I want to help." Just because you can cope alone it doesn't mean that you should.

Parents tended to be particularly attentive when a student child had experienced illness in the past. One daughter said that she understood that her mother needed to know that she was all right: 'I completely understand 'cos . . . they've got this daughter who's had problems in the past . . . make sure she's all right'.

Academic support

While the vast majority of parents had been involved in a variety of ways in the process of choosing a university (e.g., reading "personal statements" and accompanying the child to "open days"), relatively few gave substantive, hands-on help with the student's coursework or examination revision. However, one male student reported that:

> The day before my exam I was nervous obviously and actually, no, it was on the day, like an hour before my exam I rang him [father] up to . . . just say I don't know what to do, I don't know enough and he spoke to me for . . . half an hour telling me about Marx and such stuff that I didn't know, which was really helpful.

Another female student gave her mother her coursework essays to read and the mother helped her particularly with the footnotes, while two more mothers had advised their student children on coping with dyslexia, one telephoning the university to insist that more help be offered.

But most of the students mentioning 'help' with academic work had in fact sought 'reassurance', for example about their option choices. A second male student said: 'I think it's . . . weird like how you talk about things that you're thinking, just to . . . validate them', for example about an examination that he felt had not gone as well as the others: 'I'm thinking just to get them to agree with me and make me feel better'.

Filial duty

Much of the support discussed so far amounted to the parent acting as a 'sounding board', although advice was also offered *inter alia* by many, whether on how to change a light bulb, deal with a difficult room or flat mate, or format essays. But there is a further reason why many of the students kept in touch, related to the students' perceptions that their parents (or parent in the case of a lone mother) were missing them. Parents were often wary of imposing on their offspring by overly frequent telephone calls or texts, but students were also often sensitive to the fact that their parents appreciated contact. One son said: 'I'm kind of rubbish at . . . speaking to them, because I know they really want to chat and I'm usually busy', adding that he would probably not be in touch as frequently as once a week if he had not sensed that his parents wanted that level of contact. Similarly, another son, who finally settled on calling home on a Sunday, said: 'I mean partly because I want to and partly because they really appreciate it, so I sort of feel that I should. . . . They care what's happening'. A daughter who had sought and received an enormous amount of emotional support during her first term said that she continued to feel a 'duty' to call her parents, but then corrected herself, saying that it was 'nice to phone'.

There is in this, as in the evidence regarding the initiation of contact, an implicit re-negotiation of the relationship between student and parent. The vast majority of students sought some kind of support from their parents as well as 'keeping in touch' by sending 'chatty' texts or making brief telephone calls. Nevertheless, most also reached the point where they pondered the frequency of contact and tried, often after a crisis and the frequent communication with their parents that accompanied it, to moderate the number of longer telephone calls in particular. There was, nevertheless, substantial evidence of "give and take" and students tended to be sensitive to their parent's wish for regular contact.

A minority of students and parents, usually mothers and daughters, went further and talked about the fact that they wanted a relationship of 'equals', usually referring to this as becoming 'friends'. One mother said:

> I actually think when she was growing up I'd always had this dream that I would have a daughter and we'd be friends when she grew up. . . . I've always wanted to be friends with my daughter in contrast to the relationship I had with my mother really.

In this, as in many comments made by parents wanting frequent contact with their student children, there is a desire for things to be "different" from the relationship they had had with their own parents. Some mothers were in fact impatient for their daughters to become mature, independent adults, whom they could treat more as friends. However, for the students, friendship could exist alongside dependence. One male student felt that his father was his 'friend': 'I speak to my Dad like every day . . . it's just like . . . we're basically like friends . . . we laugh and joke and stuff'. Yet this student was very dependent on his father (and his mother) for all kinds of support.

The lure of home

About a quarter of parents said without prompting that they had not wanted their young adult children to go to university too far away and had helped them to choose a university by attending open days with them. For example, the South Asian parents expected their children to attend a university close to their homes. Students seemed to be content with the way in which their choices had been made, and most did not want to go too far afield; one female student said that she had wanted to be just far enough away from her home to make it difficult to return on a whim. The lure of home was strong for the majority of the students.

Almost half the parent respondents (fathers as well as mothers) referred to finding the departure of the child for university very difficult, using words such as 'bereavement' and 'grieving', and describing the separation as being 'one of the worst days ever', 'like falling off a cliff'. One mother spoke at greater length about her daughter's departure: 'It's the end of the era, I felt, as a parent. And you know that's hard. . . . I loved being a parent . . . it was painful'. Nevertheless, several of these parents had counselled their children that they must 'stick it out' when they experienced emotional crises in their first term, recognising the importance of getting a university education and achieving some degree of independence.

The vast majority of students missed their home comforts: home cooked meals, Xboxes, space (in the form of their bedrooms and gardens) and feeling safe (being protected and looked after) featured largely in their accounts. One male student said: 'Everything is organised at home, it's safer and nice for a period'. A female student said: 'It's really nice to have space . . . to be able to just walk around and not have to just live in your little room'. As some parents commented, this was markedly different from their own experience. Leaving homes that were not as comfortable, sometimes for more modern university residences, had been no great sacrifice for them.

Two things signalled the importance of home to students: first, their desire to keep their bedrooms, and second, whether they had reached the point at which they no longer automatically identified their home town as "home". More than half the students said that they were able to return to the same bedroom in the parental home. In the case of one female student, her mother was careful to keep her bedroom until after her first vacation visit. After that, one of the two remaining sisters occupied it. The student kept her own wardrobe and chest of drawers and said that the new arrangement was only sensible, but that she was a 'bit emotional' when she saw her old room with her sister in it. In the case of a male student who kept his room, his parents redecorated it, symbolising the change that had taken place. However, only four students felt that their university town and university accommodation was 'home', although an equally small number felt somewhat ambivalent about where to call home.

The vast majority continued to feel that 'home was home'. They reported feeling that home was a 'place of refuge', a 'safe haven', where they could slip easily into old routines, albeit that a few reflected on the extent to which they had separated what they did and how they lived at home from how they lived at university: 'It's . . . divided much more separately now and I just feel like I've separated what I do at home and what I do at [University], and I live both lives equally'.

Some parents were less content about the student falling back into old habits: expecting washing to be done and not offering to do the washing up. One mother referred to this as 'reverting to kid mode', while a female student who said that 'it's nice . . . doing just chilled things with my family', added that it also felt like 'I'm regressing'.

All the parents felt that they would either want or had an obligation to offer their young adult child accommodation after graduation if it proved necessary. One mother told her daughter: 'If you . . . need a break, then this is your home, you're safe here and we have no expectations'. Others were resigned to the fact that both the housing and labour markets made return likely. Another parent said that 'people should be encouraged to be independent, but it has to be an elastic sort of arrangement', a very common view. The South Asian parents were the only ones to expect and unequivocally welcome the return of their children, the norm being for children to live at home until marriage. Indeed, seven parents expressed negative feelings about 'return', saying that they would be disappointed if this were to be the case, because they saw going away to university as a rite of passage and because they feared that it would be hard to renegotiate relationships with their co-resident young adult children. Six more parents stated simply that they would prefer to live without adult children.

However, very few students said that they would feel badly or embarrassed about a need to return home, or that they would feel that they had "failed". Nor were these views held more strongly by female than male students. One male student said, 'In this . . . economic climate it's not that weird just to live with your parents after', and another said:

> I don't really see it massively as a backward step really, just because realistically. . ., it's cheap and it's nice living there . . . with my mum and dad to do things for me, which they gladly do, which is nice. Like, I'm not imposing.

These students recognised that behavioural norms were shifting, however in both cases their parents expressed the strong hope that they would live independently after leaving university. Six students said that they feared 'reverting back' to how things were before university if they returned home and referred to the possibility that their parents would still treat them as dependent children with the result that they would have less freedom. Most feared that they would stop moving forward: 'Instead of keeping moving forward you'd just feel like you've stopped' (female student). We explore the issues raised by returning graduates and their parents at greater length in Chapters 3 and 4.

Conclusion: dependence and independence

The vast majority of both students and parents wanted the former to become more independent during their years at university. However, the South Asian parents and children did not think like this, explaining that it would be 'normal' for the student to return home on graduation. In the case of one student who was attending university in his home town, the parent was keen for him to return home after only one or two years at university.

Students tended to feel more autonomous and to be more satisfied with their progress towards independent living than were their parents, highlighting how they had managed their time and social lives, as well as welcoming contact with their parents. However, there were tensions for the majority of parents, who wanted to maintain a good relationship with their children – ideally better than they had managed to achieve with their own parents – but at the same time expressed concern about the degree to which they should support their offspring. The problem of balance and of giving their student children both "roots" and "wings" (Karp et al., 2004) loomed large.

Students

On the whole, the students were not only more satisfied with the degree of independence they had achieved than their parents, but also tended to welcome contact with parents as an aid rather than a hindrance to achieving independence. Arnett's (1994) emphasis on the importance of accepting responsibility for own actions and establishing a more equal relationship with parents as markers of independence for young adults (see also Gaudet, 2001; Gillies et al., 2001; Wintre and Yaffe, 2000) was supported by our sample of students. But his suggestion that developing own values and beliefs was also important was only referred to implicitly by a very small minority who reflected on the meaning of making the transition to the adult world. As one male student put it: 'You're more driven to . . . mould yourself into the person you . . . want to be in later life . . . it's just easier to . . . find yourself'.

Rather more emphasis was put on the importance of making their own decisions, which was closely linked to taking responsibility for their own actions (as per their management of money; see Chapter 1). Many students spoke of feeling that they had more control over their lives. As one female student put it, living alone at university and thinking of her own needs and how to organise her time had been 'quite empowering'. A male student said:

> I am happy with the way I've coped, I'm happy that I didn't choose to live at home and I'm happy that I did kick on through [after an early emotional crisis] . . . . I've surprised myself by what I can do.

Most students felt that they had achieved greater autonomy – albeit that they invariably used the term independence – and most felt that having to ask for day-to-day help, for example when a bank card was stolen, should not be taken as a sign of dependence. A South Asian male student did not expect to have to do his own cooking or laundry and so did not feel that reliance on his mother in this respect was a measure of dependence. Similarly, while most recognised the degree to which they were emotionally dependent on their parents, they were still prepared to make a claim for greater independence:

> I've made it sound, I don't know, like I'm totally reliant on them. And maybe, maybe I am more than I think. . . . But no I feel . . . like I would do a lot of things for myself.

To this extent they felt that they were developing a more equal relationship with their parents, but many acknowledged the huge importance of "parent as backstop": 'But in a way, it's . . . nice to know that my parents will sort of pick up the pieces if I do find I can't do this' (female student). Even students who remained very emotionally dependent were able to report something that made them feel that they were "on the road" to independent living. One son who was in touch with his mother several times a week said: 'I think if I spoke to her every day then I wouldn't be able to fully feel like I was independent'. But several referred explicitly to being 'treated more as an adult' (female student) and 'having a bit more authority' (male student) in discussions with parents.

Some were unwilling to put dependence and independence in completely separate boxes: 'I don't need to see my parents every day. . . [but] when I'm stressed I know they'll be there for me. So in that way I've realised how dependent I am on them' (female student). Above all, students assessed the degree to which they had become more independent according to their own lights (cf. Gillies et al., 2001; Manzoni, 2016). A few students and parents spoke of the young adult becoming 'more independent-minded', with more confidence about sorting things out for him/herself. For the most part, support from parents, especially at crucial moments of crisis, was seen by students as an aid and encouragement to developing active independence and becoming more independently minded, rather than undermining it.

Parents

Almost all parents mentioned the importance of students becoming more independent and many worried about whether this was happening. But parents revealed more ambivalence about progress than their children.

Most parents wanted to see their children going "out into the world" confident, competent and happy. Several talked about their understanding of the university years as a period of transition. One mother saw it as her job to:

> manage this transition . . . the level of support we're giving her is helping her transition her way into being independent, because to go from being at home to suddenly not being at home I think . . . it's just natural that you need that . . . slight sort of easing out process. . . . I think we've taken our cues from her . . . I don't think we've really botched this one, no. . . . We haven't not given advice.

Parents tended to look for evidence of increased maturity and responsibility. One mother said that her son was not yet sufficiently independent, especially in regard to the second of these: 'He'll still come back home and you know, everything will be provided . . . life's too easy'. However, several parents also saw in their student children's willingness to ask for support a sign of greater maturity, for example the same mother also said that her son had taken her advice on time management (see also Gillies et al., 2001).

Parents also showed considerable ambivalence about the process of their children becoming independent. Some feared losing close contact with the child: 'I don't want the same distance to exist between her and me as existed between my parents and myself' (father). But they often also felt that their children should show more inclination "to get on with it": 'I don't think I'm a hard mother or an uncaring mother, it's just that I want my children to be independent'. Another mother felt that her daughter should be a 'bit more resilient . . . going to university, being taught nice things . . . it shouldn't really be that difficult'.

Ambivalence manifested itself in what were often frequent expressions of concern about the student's degree of dependence and a desire to enable autonomy (Cullaty, 2011; Gillies et al., 2001; Soenens et al., 2007; Wartman and Savage, 2008), alongside actions that did not necessarily support this goal. Thus, for example, parents expressed concern about a student child's dependence and yet initiated frequent contact, or claimed to place a high value on encouraging independence while sorting out a problem for a child. But some parents showed considerable awareness of the tensions:

> The whole thing about being a parent is that kind of dynamic between dependency and independence isn't it? . . . Your role is really bring them up to be independent. But . . . the way I've always looked at it, there's this push/pull all the time . . . The birds actually get pushed out of the nest and forced to fly. . . . So I think I do have a bit of that in me . . . saying you need to be independent. But I'm . . . on the other side. . . . I'd like her to stay at home really.
>
> (father)

However, the level of contact that parents maintained with their student children (with which the latter were generally happy) meant that they tended to be ambivalent about how far and in what ways to promote independence. The problem of securing "roots" and encouraging "wings" was real (cf. Karp et al., 2004).

No parent denied their child help at times of crises, but because these tended to occur early in the first year, there was a sense in which parents might have been on the look-out for signs of problems thereafter. But we found very little evidence of parents engaging in and regarding as acceptable the kind of controlling or directive behaviours that could be characterised as "helicopter parenting". Parents varied considerably in how far they were prepared to help their children with day-to-day activities and to provide emotional support (substantial academic support was rare), but all acknowledged the importance of the student showing signs of developing greater independence and most tried consciously to provide the kind of support that would enable autonomy and independence.

Note

1 See also West et al. (2009) for concerns regarding parents as Facebook "friends".

References

Arnett, J. (1994). Are college students adults? Their conceptions of the transition to adulthood. *Journal of Adult Development*, 1(4): 213–224.

Arnett, J. (2000). Development from the late teens through the twenties. *American Psychologist*, 55(5): 469–480.

Bellah, R., Madsen, R., Sullivan, W., Swidler, A. and Tipton, S. M. (1985). *Habits of the Heart: Middle America Observed*. Berkeley, CA: University of California Press.

Bengtson, V., Giarrusso, R., Mabry, J. and Silverstein, M. (2002). Solidarity, conflict and ambivalence: Complementary or competing perspectives on intergenerational relationships? *Journal of Marriage and Family*, 64(3): 568–576.

Cicchelli, V. and Martin, C. (2004). Young adults in France: Becoming adult in the context of increased autonomy and dependency. *Journal of Comparative Family Studies*, 35(4): 615–626.

Coburn, K. (2006, July/August). Organizing a ground crew for today's helicopter parents. *About Campus*, 9–16.

Côté, J. and Bynner, J. M. (2008). Changes in the transition to adulthood in the UK and Canada: The role of structure and agency in emerging adulthood. *Journal of Youth Studies*, 11(3): 251–268.

Cullaty, B. (2011). The role of parental involvement in the autonomy development of traditional-age college students. *Journal of College Student Development*, 52(4): 25–439.

Fingerman, K., Cheng, Y.-P., Wesselman, E., Zarit, S., Furstenburg, F. and Birditt, K. (2012). Helicopter parents and landing pad kids: Intense parental support of grown children. *Journal of Marriage and Family*, 74(4): 880–896.

Fingerman, K., Miller, L., Birditt, K. and Zarit, S. (2009). Giving to the good and the needy: Parental support of grown children. *Journal of Marriage and Family*, 71(5): 1220–1233.

Furstenberg, F., Kennedy, S., McLoyd, V. C., Rumbaut, R. G. and Settersten, R. A. (2004). Growing up is harder to do. *Contexts*, 3(3): 33–41.

Gaudet, S. (2001). La responsabilité dans les debuts de l'âge adulte. *Liens social et Politiques, Numéro*, 46(2): 71–83.

Gillies, V., McCarthy, J. and Holland, J. (2001). *"Pulling Together, Pulling Apart": The Family Lives of Young People*. York: Joseph Rowntree Foundation.

Holdsworth, C. (2009). "Going away to uni": Mobility, modernity, and independence of English higher education students. *Environment and Planning A*, 41(8): 1850–1864.

Karp, D., Holmstrom, L. and Gray, P. (2004). Of roots and wings: Letting go of the college-bound child. *Symbolic Interaction*, 27(3): 357–382.

Kenny, M. (1987). The extent and function of parental attachment among first-year college students. *Journal of Youth and Adolescence*, 16(1): 17–27.

Kloep, M. and Hendry, L. (2010). Letting go or holding on? Parents' perceptions of their relationships with their children during emerging adulthood. *British Journal of Developmental Psychology*, 28(4): 817–834.

Koepke, S. and Denissen, J. (2012). Dynamics of identity development and separation-individuation in parent-child relationships during adolescence and emerging adulthood – a conceptual integration. *Developmental Review*, 32(1): 67–88.

Manzoni, A. (2016). Conceptualizing and measuring youth independence multidimensionally in the United States. *Acta Sociologica*, 59(4): 362–377.

Newman, K. S. (2012). *The Accordion Family*. Boston, MA: Beacon Press.

Padilla-Walker, L. and Nelson, L. (2012). Black hawk down? Establishing helicopter parenting as a distinct construct from other forms of parental control during emerging adulthood. *Journal of Adolescence*, 35(5): 1177–1190.

Pillemer, K., Suitor, J., Mock, S., Sabir, M., Pardo, T. and Sechrist, J. (2007). Capturing the complexity of intergenerational relations: Exploring ambivalence with later-life families. *Journal of Social Issues*, 63(4): 775–791.

Ryan, R. and Lynch, J. (1989). Emotional autonomy versus detachment: Revisiting the vicissitudes of adolescence and young adulthood. *Child Development*, 60(2): 340–356.

Sarigiani, P., Trumbell, J. and Camarena, P. (2013). Electronic communications technologies and the transition to college: Links to parent-child attachment and adjustment. *Journal of the First-year Experience and Students in Transition*, 25(1): 35–60.

Scabini, E., Marta, E. and Lanz. M. (2006). *The Transition to Adulthood and Family Relations*. Hove: Psychology Press.

Schiffrin, H. H., Liss, M., Miles-McLean, H., Geary, K. A., Erchull, M. J. and Tashner, T. (2014). Helping or hovering? The effects of helicopter parenting on college students' well-being. *Journal of Child and Family Studies*, 23(3): 548–557.

Schultheiss, D. P. and Blustein, D. L. (1994). Contributions of family relationship factors to the identity formation process. *Journal of Counseling and Development*, 73(2): 159–166.

Settersten, R. A. (2012). The contemporary context of young adulthood in the US: From demography to development, from private troubles to public issues. In A. Booth, S. L. Brown, N. S. Landale, W. D. Manning and S. M. McHale (Eds.), *Early Adulthood in a Family Contest* (pp. 3–26). New York: Springer.

Soenens, B., Vansteenkiste, M., Lens, W., Luyckx, K., Goossens, L., Byers, W. and Ryan, R. M. (2007). Conceptualizing parental autonomy support: Perceptions of promotion of independence versus promotion of volitional functioning. *Developmental Psychology*, 43(3): 633–646.

Sorokou, C. and Weissbrod, C. (2005). Men and women's attachment and contact patterns with parents during the first year of college. *Journal of Youth and Adolescence*, 34(3): 221–228.

Spence, P. (2012). *Parental involvement in the lives of college students: Impact on student independence, self-direction, and critical thinking*. Dissertations, Paper 315. Chicago: Loyola University.

Stein, C. H., Osborn, L. A. and Greenberg, S. C. (2016). Understanding young adults' reports of contact with their parents in a digital world: Psychological and familial relationship factors. *Journal of Child and Family Studies*, 25(6): 1802–1814.

Wartman, K. and Savage, M. (2008). *Parental involvement in higher education: Understanding the relationship among students, parents and the institution.* Higher Education Report Series, 33(6). San Francisco, CA: Association for the Study of Higher Education.

West, A., Lewis, J. and Currie, P. (2009). Students' Facebook 'friends': Public and private spheres. *Journal of Youth Studies*, 12(6): 615–627.

Whittington, L. and Peters, H. (1996). Economic incentives for financial and residential independence. *Demography*, 33(1): 82–97.

Wintre, M. and Yaffe, M. (2000). First-year students' adjustment to university life as a function of relationship with parents. *Journal of Adolescent Research*, 15(1): 9–38.

3 Co-resident graduates and parents
Relationships, jobs and future expectations

Introduction

As we have seen, student children and parents tend to be closer than in previous generations. It is now also increasingly common for graduate children to return to the parental home, something that had been unusual for their parents. While it may be that returning to live at home is becoming a "new norm" (see also Stone et al., 2014), it is reasonable to assume that "returning" may pose challenges for both graduates and their parents, who may well feel that successful parenting involves "launching" the child into the outside world.

The national media have tended to emphasise the problems faced by parents and their young adult "boomerang" children who return home (e.g., Cummings, 2013; Koslow and Booth, 2012; Utley, 2016), but academic (usually quantitative) analysis based on North American data has often been more equivocal and sometimes considerably more positive (e.g., Aquilino and Supple, 1991; Mitchell, 1998; Parker, 2012; Sassler et al., 2008). In this study, we use qualitative data from parents and co-resident graduates to explore the experience of both graduates returning to the parental home and one of their parents (see Introduction).

In Chapter 2 we saw that the students in our first sample anticipated the need to return home with relative equanimity; only a few expressed concerns about losing independence if they did so. A majority of their parents were clearly in favour of their student children not returning home if at all possible. This chapter begins by outlining our overall approach and then investigating how our second sample of graduates and their parents felt about the return home and what the reasons for it were. We go on to discuss the relationship between co-resident parent and child, focusing on how close each feels to the other, how far both felt that the graduate had come to occupy a more "adult" place in the household, and the points of tension, for example, contributions to household chores. The chapter then considers the issue of job status for the graduates and the parents. Even though these parents and children had volunteered to participate in the study and might therefore be expected to get on fairly well, we found considerable tensions and ambivalence, more on the part of the parents than the graduates. Finally, we consider the expectations graduates and parents have for leaving home, and offer further observations on the vexed issue of young adults achieving independence.

Our approach

For both graduates and parents, a return home can appear as a backward step running counter to expectations of advance into full adulthood. Perhaps it is not surprising that much of the quantitative evidence on "return" has focused on whether or not parents and young adult children are "satisfied" with the experience. There were often tensions in the relationships, but as more recent literature has argued, there may also be ambiguity in the feelings of parents and children. Achievement of independence remained an important goal for both parties – albeit that once again it is understood somewhat differently – and we draw again on the psychological and sociological literature pertaining to this.

Satisfaction and dissatisfaction with co-residence

Taking a young adult back into the parental home appears to exemplify family solidarity. However, this does not in and of itself guarantee satisfaction with the situation. Early quantitative US research found that most parents did not welcome the return of a child (Umberson, 1992). However, there is now rather more evidence (from the US and Canada) of relatively high levels of satisfaction on the part of parents and children (Aquilino and Supple, 1991; Mitchell, 1998; Parker, 2012; Wister et al., 1997). Using qualitative data, Sassler et al. (2008) found that almost three-quarters of their sample of 30 young adult 'returners' in southern New England were positive about their experiences.

Previous quantitative work has also suggested that it might not be co-residence *per se* that affects the levels of satisfaction of parent and child. Rather, the adult child's problems, especially continued economic dependence, were found to be associated with parental dissatisfaction (Aquilino, 1991). Aquilino (1999) also concluded that there were systematic differences in the perspectives of parents and adult children.

Ambivalence

In 1998, Luescher and Pillemer proposed that ambivalence might be as, or more, important a category for analysis as satisfaction (see also Fingerman et al., 2004; Willson et al., 2003), that is: how far both positive and negative evaluations of a relationship are held simultaneously. Some qualitative work has reported parents having positive feelings which existed alongside conflict (Dor, 2013), and returners saying that they felt both autonomous and dependent in relation to some issues (Molgat, 2007; see also Cicchelli and Martin, 2004). But there has been little agreement as to the importance of ambivalence.

However, as Furlong and Cartmel (1997) have commented, it is not surprising that returners may feel both an entitlement to return to the parental home and resentment about the need for it, while Pillemer and Suitor (2002; also Pillemer et al., 2007) have pointed out that parents may experience conflict between their wish to help their children and the expectation that children will make progress towards full independence. The return to co-residence entails dependence and its duration is usually unknown, which can undermine the idea of steady progress towards independence and make ambivalence more likely (Pillemer and Suitor, 2002). As Smelser (1997: 8) observed, 'dependent situations' – in which the structural conditions offer fewer escape options – may 'breed ambivalence' (see also Birditt et al., 2009; Connidis and McMullin, 2002). We show that ambivalence is important for understanding the implications of an additional period of co-residence, especially for parents.

Achieving independence

Arnett (2000, 2006) characterised his much debated identification of a new developmental stage – covering those in their late teens and twenties (particularly 18- to 25-year-olds) – as the period of life that has become the 'most volitional' of all (2000: 465), with 'self-focused' 'emerging adults' able to try out options in terms of work and relationships. In respect of returning to the parental home, it is interesting that studies have signalled the importance of whether the returner actively *chose* to return home (Kohli and Albertini, 2008), linking this to the degree of satisfaction felt by young adult co-residents (Kins et al., 2009).

Arnett has stressed the importance of informal and intangible psychological criteria, and as we have already seen, his empirical work with 'emerging adults' identified individualistic criteria for achieving adulthood, including taking responsibility for self, and establishing a relationship with parents as an equal adult (see also Sassler et al., 2008), as well as financial independence (Arnett, 2001). We shall discuss the importance of these criteria for both the graduates and their parents, whose perspectives may differ. For example, co-residence may be perceived to bring with it issues of responsibility to others (e.g., Gillies et al., 2001) as well as the responsibility-for-self stressed by Arnett (2001).

However, adult independence has usually been defined in terms of formal, tangible transitions, particularly the availability of independent housing and jobs, for young people (e.g., Settersten and Ray, 2010). Côté and Bynner (2008) have argued that young people must react to the situation they find themselves in and 'cope', rather than make unfettered choices; in other words, they may find it difficult to exercise agency. Given that the state of the labour market and housing costs have been shown to be important in accounting for a return to the parental home (see Introduction), it would be difficult to dismiss the importance of context.

Concern about achieving autonomy and independence is sharpened for parents and co-resident graduates, and brings with it the possibility of heightened day-to-day tensions. We consider the extent to which the young adult feels able to and is perceived to be capable of taking his or her place as an equal member of the household, for example, by expressing own opinions, but also by contributing to the household. For graduates, living with parents is likely to be due in large part to lack of financial independence, occasioned by unemployment, under-employment or lack of a sufficiently well-paying job (to pay a market rent or mortgage), which may elicit different degrees of concern from parents and children (as well as different amounts of material assistance on the part of the former; see Chapter 4). In addition, parents and adult children may or may not share goals and timetables for achieving greater independence.

Our sample comprised 27 parents and co-resident graduates, with 54 interviewees in total (see Introduction). Graduates had lived with their parents for between three months and seven and a half years (mean 22 months).

Returning home

The majority of graduates knew what to expect when they returned home. However, for some there had been fundamental changes in the position of their parents. For two, the fathers had been made redundant, and for three the parents had divorced. These new situations meant a "new start" had to be made, which in some cases intensified the tensions around returning and in others made return easier. For example, one graduate had not intended to live in her parental home, now occupied by only her divorced father, and at the beginning she had felt disoriented; but she described how, within a few months, she began to build a new relationship with her father: 'It was like we were both finding out how to do something new together, so it didn't feel, like, oppressive, or anything like that'. The remaining graduates returned home to either their childhood bedroom – 'the same room I was in for the last ten years' – or a smaller one because a sibling had moved up in the "bedroom hierarchy" (see also Chapter 2), something one parent found to be a source of constant irritation between her children. A divorced mother had had to 'downsize' and there were some difficulties in accommodating the graduate and the mother's new partner in a much smaller flat.

Four graduates in our sample stressed that they chose to return (see also Kohli and Albertini, 2008) because it made their intensive and extensive (and often long) job search easier. However, five female graduates returned home 'without really thinking about it'. Most of these said that they liked living at home and felt no stigma in so doing, and several said that they would not want to live alone. One said simply: 'Home is the place I feel most comfortable in the world probably'.

A larger group said that they had felt that return was 'inevitable' and that they had not 'minded it'. It was also common for members of this group of graduates to have felt somewhat disinclined to return at first, but to have quickly adjusted, reporting that it had 'made sense': 'I don't think it would have been my first choice to come back home, but it was the most sensible option in the end'. Included in this group were the four South Asian males in the sample, for whom returning home after graduation was expected, and who all accepted the cultural norm.

There was also a small group of five graduates who felt that return had been inevitable, but who expressed profound dissatisfaction with their position. One stressed that she had not chosen to return, and described her return as a 'retreat' after 'failure'; her employment plans had collapsed. For some of these graduates, returning home was initially a welcome change: 'everything at home is clean and food tastes good at home and someone washes your clothes and it's novel, so it kind of felt like being in a hotel for a bit' (female graduate), but after a few months these graduates came to despair of their living arrangements. Two spoke eloquently about the 'whole stigma of living with your parents'.

Parents, for the most part, were philosophical about the need to return: 'It's not a matter of allowing it [return], it just happens'. They recognised that their young adult children had a 'completely different mind-set' about return to the one they had held at a similar age. But two parents said that from the beginning they had been concerned that home might be too comfortable and adversely affect progression to full independence: 'It's comfort as well to be honest . . . he gets food, unlimited TV and a floor [in the house] to himself' (father).

Certainly, there was tension between a significant minority of parents and children about how far the graduate child had a 'right' to return home. Six graduates said that while they felt they had a 'right to return', it could be conditional (see also White, 2002). Eight graduates expressed the view that they had an unconditional right of return:

> I still see this place as my home and because I think having a home is really important, so . . . until you've made a new home . . . the feeling that your family home is your home is quite important for a long time.
>
> (female graduate)

This group of respondents found any suggestion that they might not have an unconditional right to return 'hurtful', 'hard to swallow'.

All parents felt that they had some obligation to provide 'a roof' or 'safety net' for their graduate children. One mother said that this was 'the mentality of everybody around here. . . . I think if I said "Oh, we're not having [our son] back", I think you would be mad . . . people would think I was very strange', a comment that infers the extent to which 'returning' was already normative for some White British respondents. Others referred to the way in which they had been 'lucky' when they had left university, but that 'times are tough' for their children. A few referred to the need for the parent to continue to provide 'a safe nurturing space from which they can launch themselves into the world. . . . That's what you do' (mother) – even when, as in this case, the tensions between parent and child over everyday living were extreme.

However, the vast majority of parents also felt that 'there is no blank cheque'. Parents talked about the need for balance: the graduate child should 'reciprocate' in some way by doing household chores, by 'being nice and helpful', and by applying assiduously for jobs. When asked about obligations, ten parents mentioned reciprocity in terms of 'care' for them in old age. This was normative in the case of the South Asian parents and children. It was perhaps more significant in respect of the White British respondents. Several were not necessarily hoping for 'hands-on care', but rather for children 'to keep an eye on us', or to help out financially with care costs. One father made a clear (and spontaneous) statement as to how he viewed the intergenerational contract: 'I think the contract I feel between me and her is . . . I look after you now when you're young and you look after me when I'm old. That's how I hope things will turn out'. Only one graduate explicitly mentioned the possibility of offering help to parents in their old age.

On the whole, the parents expressed more ambivalence about their graduate children's return. While many said that there were many things to like about 'having him/her around', their focus on the conditional nature of return indicated anxieties about the child's ability and willingness to develop and move on. The graduates did not see as much risk in returning, viewing it more as an inevitable step along the way, but there were considerable differences as to how positive or negative they felt about it.

Relationships between graduates and parents

As in the case of the student sample, parents and graduates tended to describe their relationship as close, sometimes even when there was considerable tension. Some of the graduates were careful to distinguish between their feelings for their family and about living at home. Thus, a female graduate said that she was grateful to her parents, but was very unhappy: 'I need to not be living at home!' However, for a small minority of graduates, their 'situation' – in the form of their place in the family home, coping with domestic routines, identity crises and joblessness – resulted in acute unhappiness, which became inseparable from their feelings about their relationships with their parents. For their part, parents struggled with uncertainty about the duration of the graduate child's return, and focused most of their attention on the contributions of their graduate children to the household, their commitment to job search and whether they were taking on more responsibility and behaving in a more adult way.

Closeness and graduates' position in the household

The vast majority of graduates articulated less concern about their relationship with their parents than did the parents. In three cases, the graduate felt that the family dynamic had changed since he or she had left for university, and that they were able to 'mediate' in parental disputes: 'I know that I'm important in, yeah, keeping my parents, like happy' (female graduate). Another small minority felt that they were becoming more like 'friends' with their parents (see also Chapter 2), although their parents did not always agree, while a similar number felt differently, stressing that the parental home belonged to their parents: 'it's not a shared house'.

In many ways closeness to parents was strongly related to how far the graduate felt that it had been possible to occupy a 'more equal adult role' in the household. Graduates found this quite difficult to talk about; it was fundamentally difficult to claim to be a fully independent adult while living at home. A very few, males and females, declared that they felt 'more grown up now' or were 'pretty much an adult now', albeit that they were unable to offer much evidence of this, and not all their parents agreed. Still, almost all could point to something that they felt indicated progress, for example, the feeling that they could contribute to adult conversations about 'houses and politics', or argued less with parents, who respected their opinions more.

A majority of graduates stressed the importance of whether they were 'respected' by their parents and treated more as adults (Arnett, 2001). However, most graduates felt that any progress towards adulthood in this regard had been counter-balanced by a loss of the freedom and social independence they had enjoyed as students. Seven graduates felt that they were not given the respect due to an adult, and four very strongly so: 'My parents are particularly unwilling, I think, to know me as an adult . . . they're still holding onto the image they have of me as a child' (male graduate).

While graduates were primarily concerned about 'moving on' in their relationship with parents, parents were most concerned about the extent to which the young adult child was demonstrating more 'adult behaviour'. Ten parents said that they had continued to treat their graduate offspring as children, something that most were not happy about. However, some found it inevitable, in one case because the daughter had to be nagged to do things, while in another a mother said of her son: 'I'm trying to give him enough space to be an adult. . . . I think the most important thing is not to nag, not to ask, accept he's an adult', but she felt that her son was not behaving 'responsibly'. Nevertheless, a few parents expressed strong feelings about the fundamental importance of continuing to build and retain close relationships with their children. One mother commented:

> Our understanding is that [our son] doesn't want to be with us any longer than he need be. But he knows that . . . it can always be a home base. . . . It's not for ever and having a good relationship with your children is the most important thing.

The need for a new kind of "balancing act" (see also Chapter 2) was recognised by the parents of graduates. Only one parent, a father, said that the graduate child had shown such a lack of progress in taking on more responsibilities and demonstrating more adult behaviour that he thought that 'my relationship with her would have been much better if she had left'. In this case the daughter's regression to teenage behaviour constituted a threat to the relationship.

Contributions to the household and 'taking responsibility'

Parents expected graduates to engage with domestic routines which were often similar to those they had experienced as children, and parents' ideas about responsible behaviour might not allow for eating toast late at night or leaving dirty dishes in the sink, for example. Some graduates coped with such restrictions better than others.

In a very few cases, graduates did very little or nothing by way of household chores, but this was not necessarily a problem for their parents. A female graduate living with her father reported that she did very little but that '[her father was] an angel . . . I am just lazy . . . he never complains'. All but one of the South Asian graduates (and their parents) accepted that it was the mother's job, together with any co-resident aunts and grandmothers, to do the domestic work. Two female graduates admitted to doing little, but felt that whatever they did to contribute, they could not 'quite win'. If they cooked or cleaned, then they would be told that they had not done so to the required standard.

Furthermore, a substantial majority of graduates did not really see why they should do much by way of housework. A female graduate who had felt strongly entitled to return to the parental home also felt that she should be able to concentrate on building her career. Another reported that she was nagged about doing chores, which she found 'annoying'. She confessed to being lazy: her parents left her a 'to do' list which consisted of things that she should probably 'think of to do, but I just don't, so. . .'. Many of these graduates knew that they had 'regressed' and said so without prompting. But in two cases, including the young woman who was 'annoyed' by the nagging, the graduates did not see their lack of engagement with or responsibility for household work as threatening their advance to full adult independence: 'I don't think I've lost the ability to turn on the washing machine or anything, so I don't think it matters particularly'. This female graduate went on to say that 'at home I choose to be less independent and it's kind of easier to have someone to tell you to do things'.

Parents, fathers as much as mothers, tended to express considerable frustration about the tendency of their graduate children to regress into previous, teenage patterns of behaviour, falling back into old routines, contributing little and needing prompting to do things. One mother said: 'It is a sort of continuation . . . I suppose you could say we, sort of slipped back into the old routine'. A second mother said that her son did not contribute much, he would vacuum, but 'not necessarily the day I've asked him . . . I might quietly seethe'. A third said that she had been building her career during her child's university years and felt that the graduate failed to appreciate this. Yet another was bitter:

> I am basically number one slave. . . . I know that she doesn't know how to clean, so what I would want is the response: "OK mum, I will do that. I don't know how to clean. You show me how to clean and I will learn", because you see . . . I want her to clean it to my standards.
>
> (see also Seiffge- Kenke, 2013)

A father endorsed the view that the behaviour of his graduate daughter was not that of a responsible adult:

> She still comes home expecting her dinner to be on the table and . . . that's not necessarily appropriate in somebody of that age. . . . Every now and then she will clean the kitchen and assume this kind of aura of someone who's very . . . responsible.

These parents confirmed the view of some adult children that even when the child did contribute to household work, it was felt that this was either not up to standard, or not enough.

Fathers in particular stressed the importance of taking responsibility in terms of taking responsibility for self. Four mentioned that a son or daughter had failed to complete an insurance form after having something stolen. One father commented: 'You think, how would they . . . cope on their own'. More parents expressed frustration with what they saw as the lack of progress towards adulthood than empathised with the young adult's views of their situation. Interestingly, there was a conspicuous lack of attempts to negotiate a more harmonious division of household work. One parent commented that there was only negotiation in a 'crisis' and most parents sought to avoid those.

Problems of social constraints for graduates and life course issues for parents

A majority of graduates, and almost all the young men, thought that their social lives were constrained and often felt that they could not "be who they wanted to be".

One female graduate said that she had lost (social) independence even though she felt that her relationship with her parents was on a more equal footing. Several who were not earning, or not earning much, could not afford to go out, especially when it involved travel to meet former university friends. The difficulties of socialising after the freedom of university life were keenly felt. Some chafed at having to say whether they would be home for dinner, for example, although most accepted that this was a matter of courtesy. Two male graduates felt that they had difficulties being themselves in the company of their parents, for example, a South Asian man said: 'I'm a different person when I'm at home with my family . . . when my friends come over they always say "you're so quiet", it's really weird'. For these graduates, the prevailing feeling was one of time passing and of "missing out" on youthful pleasures. A few could reconcile themselves to the situation: it was not for ever. But feelings were strongest and most negative among those who did not have a job and could not see a way out. A female graduate made a particularly poignant comment on the extent to which she felt that she had to fit in with her parents' lifestyles and wishes: 'I just feel I have to be, kind of, a, like, filtered version of me'. Another unemployed female graduate said simply: 'When I live with my parents I feel pathetic. It feels terrible'.

Usually, parents were aware of their adult children's dissatisfaction or unhappiness, but were also concerned about the implications of the return of their children for their own lives, for example, the mothers who expressed frustration and even bitterness about having to pick up housework for a child again. Parents also wanted to have more privacy, as one father said: 'There comes a point where your parents have done their bit and it's time to let them have space as well' (see also Umberson, 1992). Similarly, a mother said that she did not want to watch television with her daughter any more, they were no longer in 'family mode'.

On the whole, parents had more problems than graduates with co-residence; a significant number expressed considerable dissatisfaction. One mother concluded wryly: 'Oh well, . . . it's not forever is it? Hopefully'. Returning home may be characterised as an inherently tense situation, due above all to uncertainty about the prospects of the young adult and the duration of co-residence.

Jobs

Jobs, or more precisely the lack of "graduate jobs", were often fundamental to how graduates felt about themselves and to how anxious the parent felt about the young adult child's future. Parents were able to rationalise the situation, for example: 'Ten years ago my children would have gone to school, gone to university and gone and got jobs. However the reality isn't quite like that, so it all takes longer', but they still worried about whether moving back home disincentivised the young adult child from pursuing a career and an independent life. Issues to do with job search in particular often underlay or exacerbated the difficulties experienced by some parents and graduates.

In terms of jobs, while only five graduates had been employed full-time on initial return home, 18 were in full-time work by the time of interview; and whereas six were unemployed on return, only one remained completely without work at the time of interview, although another had only an unpaid internship. However, it is also important to know whether the jobs were perceived as a step forward in the graduate's chosen career, or whether they were undertaken only to earn money and/or fill-in time. Only three graduates had a "career job" when they returned home, whereas 14 had achieved this goal by the time of interview. But, while only four had temporary work when they first returned, eight had work of this kind by the time of interview. The significant number of graduates (nine) who were continuing to study when they returned home (usually for master's level degrees) had dropped to three by the time of interview.

There was only one graduate who did not have a graduate job and who was entirely satisfied with her situation. However, her temporary job was strongly related to the kind of work she wanted to do in the longer term. Above all, graduates stressed the importance of parental support *vis à vis* job search. One graduate felt that because her mother had experienced unemployment, she had been very sympathetic to the difficulties her daughter was experiencing in finding appropriate, full-time employment. Another described the way in which his mother had supported his strategy of intensive job search over a year, despite his father having told him to take any sort of job. These examples bore out the idea that the goal of independence could become a 'joint enterprise' of parent and child (Scabini et al., 2006), and contrasted starkly with that of a graduate who was also told by her mother to 'just take any job', which in the daughter's view showed that 'she's [the mother] never really taken an interest in what it is that I want do to'.

Graduates with poor-quality temporary jobs, often in shops or pubs, and the graduate without any employment usually expressed considerable anxiety and frustration. One who had anticipated getting a job in 'the creative industries' referred to her 'dashed expectations'. Living at home was 'like the embodiment of my kind of, unexpected failure, if you will . . . I've been kind of crippled by it'. Parents were sometimes impatient with the situation and the efforts their offspring were making to get a job:

> It's very frustrating to see a son that sits at home . . . it can go weeks and then you'll suddenly say "well, have you applied for anything. . .?" I don't want to say every day: "Well what have you applied for today?" I've tried that.

While there is no doubt that getting a job that could be viewed at least as a stepping stone to the kind of employment they wanted to do made a huge difference as to how the graduates felt about themselves and gave them hopes for the future, it did not necessarily signal the end of co-residence. Thus the graduate whose mother had supported his strategy of intensive job search over a year was still struggling to arrange a flat-share.

Most parents were above all ambivalent. Even some of the most anxious and frustrated stressed that they did not want to force their children into work that they really did not want to do. One mother said that offering job advice was always a matter of 'feeling like you're treading a bit on egg shells, because I didn't want to force them into something that actually, . . . wasn't right for them anyway'. A second acknowledged that she was 'impatient', but added that 'there's nothing worse than being in a job that you don't like'. A third mother was sympathetic to her daughter's sense of failure: 'She's a highly creative person . . . we're very modern parents. . . . We don't put any pressure on them to do anything other than follow their natural bent, their natural inclinations', but heartily disliked the tensions that followed from the daughter's lack of employment and wondered how long the situation would last.

Expectations

Expectations were a crucial determinant of the degree of satisfaction or anxiety expressed by graduates and parents. No graduate wanted to remain dependent on parents forever. However, the strength of feeling about the situation and the level of anxiety, frustration, impatience or optimism about the future varied hugely. Parents tended to be more anxious than optimistic. They feared how long the young adult child might have to stay and what the implications might be for themselves and for any younger children in their turn. Some were explicit in recognising that they were in 'uncharted territory' and that this in and of itself provoked anxiety.

There was a small group of female graduates who were happy to return home and, while they all wanted to move out at some point, were in no hurry to leave; as one put it: 'I'm comfortable where I am'. Another said that she would not be the person she wanted to be if she was at home for ten years, but then changed this to five. This group appreciated 'home comforts' and were usually not contributing much to the work of the household.

A majority, including some who were satisfied with living at home and some who detested it, had some idea as to how long they were prepared to stay. Settersten's (1998) study of adults in Chicago found that virtually all agreed that men and women should leave home between the ages of 18 and 25. A majority of our sample also agreed on the mid-20s as the age by which they wanted to be living independently, but the notion of an age deadline was not fixed (see also Liefbroer and Billari, 2010). One female graduate said: 'I think it's a little bit weird if you're living at home after about like 25/26'. Another said that there would come a point when she 'would feel embarrassed to live at home'. For a third, the prospect of still being at home when her younger sister returned from university made her feel 'dreadful'. A group of five, including the South Asian male graduates, felt 'alright' about being at home longer because it was enabling saving.

Indeed, graduates often mentioned that other people they had known at university had also returned home. This lessened the stigma, but the practice of 'return' had *no normative shape*, other than for the South Asian graduates and their parents, who fully expected to live together until the former married. Parents felt the uncertainty of the situation more strongly than their offspring and found it difficult to reconcile the lack of a clear plan for the future with their feelings that they had an obligation to continue to offer help.

The majority of parents recognised that their adult children might continue to need to be co-resident, but ranged from the few who faced this with equanimity, to another small group who were very anxious for their children to move out as soon as possible, and a large number who were anxious above all to have a timetable for moving out. In the case of the first group, the parents were not without concern about the situation, but tended to think as much about the effect of anxieties arising from uncertainty on the child as on themselves. One mother recognised that her son did not want to be living at home and was doing his best to leave: 'It's a waiting room in some ways for him. A comfortable waiting room . . . but he doesn't know when the train is coming, so to speak'.

The group of parents who wanted their young adult children to leave as soon as possible were usually worried that home was too 'comfortable'. One mother said that while she had expected her daughter to return 'for a bit . . . the longer she's here [two and half years at the time of interview] the more I think well why on earth would she ever move out really . . . because it is so convenient and so easy'.

But above all, parents wanted "a plan". Crucially, as one mother said: 'If something appears to be temporary and everyone knows where they're going, it's very different from we don't know where this is going'. Parents wanted a "roadmap". The parents who were less anxious about co-residence still felt that it was not good for young adults to be living at home for a long period; one or two years was alright, but as one mother said: 'Oh God, not ten years from now, please!'

Discussion and conclusion

Just over half the graduates and two-thirds of the parents expressed mainly or, in a small minority of cases, wholly negative feelings about co-residence. Nevertheless, our sample of well-educated young adult children was more positive than might have been expected. This might be explained by their difficult economic circumstances, and the extent to which their peers had also had to return home. Certainly most graduates and their parents would have agreed that co-residence resulted more from changes in the job and housing markets than from choice (cf. Côté and Bynner, 2008; Settersten and Ray, 2010). We should also note that there were more female graduates in our sample than males, and that daughters tended to be more positive about more aspects of returning home, some slipping back easily into their old teenage patterns of behaviour. Nevertheless, some graduates expressed extremely negative feelings about their situation, which often meant that they resented the need to return home, while expressing the view that they were entitled to do so (see also Furlong and Cartmel, 1997).

Many parents expressed feelings that were fundamentally ambivalent, in that they acknowledged an obligation to provide a safety net for their children, while continuing to feel that both their skills as a parent and their child's successful 'launch' demanded that a move to independent living be achieved as quickly as possible. In the short term, most expected something in return for the support they provided by way of 'adult behaviour'. In particular, parents looked for evidence that the child had become more responsible, but in the most problematic cases found themselves living with young adults who showed little sign of change.

Ambivalence thrives in situations where there are not only relations of dependence but also uncertainty as to duration (Pillemer and Suitor, 2002). In addition, another period of co-residence, while increasingly common, crucially lacks any common understanding as to the norms that might govern it. Graduates tended to be more phlegmatic than their parents about how long they might stay at home, either because they recognised from the outset that finding a job and somewhere to live would not be easy, or because they liked living at home. However, while a large group of graduates were prepared to treat another period of co-residence as a means to an end, enabling as it did a period of extensive job search and sometimes saving, they were nonetheless often anxious and impatient to 'move on'.

For a small group of graduates, the need to return to the parental home for an indeterminate period of time had come as a very unwelcome shock and was a source of considerable tension between parent and child. If the child had secured a temporary or permanent graduate job, the parent usually expressed less anxiety. There was light at the end of the tunnel. Above all, many parents were eager to have some sense that there was a plan and a timetable for moving out. They were also very aware of the model that might be set for younger siblings, and the implications for their own expectations of the 'post-children' phase of their lives.

Ambivalence is a good way of characterising the overall feelings of graduates and their parents, whether their experiences of co-residence were mainly positive or mainly negative. However day-to-day, tensions about the prospects of achieving different dimensions of independence, which in a few extreme cases came close to conflict, characterised the experience of a majority of parents and a little over half the graduates. In many respects the feelings of parents came close to realising the fears expressed by the sample of parents about the possible return of their student children described at the end of Chapter 2. The majority of graduates felt that they had traded the social freedoms enjoyed at university for what was often only a little more economic independence. Thus they remained 'semi-dependent'. For those without jobs or with only temporary, poorly paid, part-time work and without the possibility of re-joining the friendship groups of their adolescence, perceptions of their situation were often that they had lost rather than gained autonomy and independence.

In respect of Arnett's (2001) individualistic criteria for achieving adulthood, considerable support was provided by our sample for the importance attributed to taking responsibility for self and achieving an equal adult status to parents. The graduates, male and female, who felt negative about co-residence tended to complain that they were not treated as adult, that their opinions were not given equal weight in the household, and that they were unable to 'be themselves' in the family home – to be an autonomous adult. Sassler et al. (2008: 286) also reported that many of their young adult respondents struggled 'to have their opinions and decisions respected by parents'. However, a significant minority of parents who were negative about co-residence mentioned their struggle not to treat their offspring as a child. This was because in their eyes the graduate was not 'taking responsibility', either for self or for others living in the household. Mitchell (1998) also found that mothers in particular were unhappy about resuming the household chores they associated with a younger child, while Sassler et al. (2008) reported conflict between parents and children over the standards to which tasks had to be performed. For their part, a significant minority of graduates expressed impatience with the idea that performance of household tasks demonstrated adult responsibility and a capacity to live independently. Furthermore, negotiation of these issues proved elusive.

Above all, there was the problem of uncertainty in terms of how to *manage* return and how long it might last. Uncertainty loomed large for the vast majority of parents and many graduates. Even when co-residence was felt to be wholly or reasonably positive, returning home had some inbuilt tensions for a large majority of graduates and all parents other than the South Asians, for whom it was normative. Achieving a balance between offering shelter and promoting independence proved difficult for a majority of parents.

Where does this leave us on the vexed issue of 'progress towards independence'? While those graduates not in career jobs felt rather bleak about their situation in the short term, more significant for the future of this middle-class group of graduates and their parents was the *time* that further parental support provided the former to search for the kind of job they wanted, and to save (see Chapter 4), even though many parents were anxious as to whether their child's 'dream job' would be obtainable. If returning home had been impossible, the situation of this group of graduates would have been much more difficult. As Newman (2012: 196) has commented, 'for the middle class . . . family represents both a haven in the heartless world of market pressures and a springboard to a more prestigious future' (see also Furstenberg et al., 2004). Furthermore, many parents and graduates took comfort from the fact that other people they knew were in the same situation, which raises the possibility that returning home after graduation may become more widely accepted and no longer subject to terms such as "boomerang children", making its management somewhat easier.

References

Aquilino, W. S. (1991). Predicting parents' experiences with co-resident adult children. *Journal of Family Issues*, 12(3): 323–342.

Aquilino, W. S. (1999).Two views of one relationship: Comparing parents' and young adult children's reports of the quality of intergenerational relations. *Journal of Marriage and Family*, 61(4): 858–870.

Aquilino, W. S. and Supple, K. R. (1991). Parent-child relations and parent's [sic] satisfaction with living arrangements when adult children live at home. *Journal of Marriage and Family*, 53(1): 13–27.

Arnett, J. J. (2000). Emerging adulthood: A theory of development from the late teens through the twenties. *American Psychologist*, 55(5): 469–480.

Arnett, J. J. (2001). Conceptions of the transition to adulthood: Perspectives from adolescence through midlife. *Journal of Adult Development*, 8(2): 133–143.

Arnett, J. J. (2006). *Emerging Adulthood: The Winding Road From the Late Teens Through the Twenties*. Oxford: Oxford University Press.

Birditt, K., Miller, L. M., Fingerman, K. L. and Lefkowitz, E. S. (2009). Tensions in the parent and adult child relationship: Links to solidarity and ambivalence. *Psychology and Aging*, 24(2): 287–295.

Cicchelli, V. and Martin, C. (2004). Young adults in France: Becoming adult in the context of increased autonomy and dependency. *Journal of Comparative Family Studies*, 35(4): 615–626.

Connidis, I. and McMullin, J. (2002). Ambivalence and family ties: A critical perspective. *Journal of Marriage and Family*, 64(3): 558–667.

Côté, J. and Bynner, J. M. (2008). Changes in the transition to adulthood in the UK and Canada: The role of structure and agency in emerging adulthood. *Journal of Youth Studies*, 11(3): 251–268.

Cummings, E. (2013, August 19). Boomerang generation: The young adults living back with parents. *The Telegraph*.

Dor, A. (2013). Don't stay out late! Mom, I'm twenty-eight: Emerging adults and their parents under one roof. *International Journal of Social Science Studies*, 1(1): 37–46.

Fingerman, K. L., Hay, E. L. and Birditt, K. S. (2004). The best of ties, the worst of ties: Close, problematic and ambivalent social relationships. *Journal of Marriage and Family*, 66(3): 792–808.

Furlong, A. and Cartmel, F. (1997). *Young People and Social Change: Individualisation and Risk in Late Modernity*. Buckingham: Open University Press.

Furstenberg, F., Kennedy, S., McLloyd, V. C., Rumbaut, R. G. and Settersten, R. A. (2004). Growing up is harder to do. *Contexts*, 3(3): 33–41.

Gillies, V., McCarthy, J. and Holland, J. (2001). *"Pulling Together, Pulling Apart": The Family Lives of Young People*. York: Joseph Rowntree Foundation.

Kins, E., Beyers, W., Soenens, B. and Vansteenkiste, M. (2009). Patterns of home leaving and subjective well-being: The role of motivational processes and parental autonomy support. *Developmental Psychology*, 45(5): 1416–1429.

Kohli, M. and Albertini, M. (2008). The family as a source of support for adult children's own family projects: European varieties. In C. Saraceno (Ed.), *Families, Ageing and Social Policy: Intergenerational Solidarity in European Welfare State* (pp. 38–58). Cheltenham: Edward Elgar.

Koslow, S. and Booth, H. (2012, August 12). Generation boomerang: Children who go back to mum and dad. *The Guardian*. Retrieved from: www.theguardian.com/lifeandstyle/2012/aug/24/generation-boomerang-adultscents

Liefbroer, A. C. and Billari, F. C. (2010). Bringing norms back in: A theoretical and empirical discussion of their importance for understanding demographic behaviour. *Population, Space and Place*, 16(3): 287–305.

Luescher, K. and Pillemer, K. (1998). A new approach to the study of parent-child relations in later life. *Journal of Marriage and Family*, 60(2): 413–425.

Mitchell, B. A. (1998). Too close for comfort? Parental assessments of 'boomerang kid' living arrangements. *The Canadian Journal of Sociology*, 23(1): 21–46.

Molgat, M. (2007). Do transitions and social structures matter? How 'emerging adults' define themselves as adults. *Journal of Youth Studies*, 10(5): 495–516.

Newman, K. S. (2012). *The Accordion Family*. Boston, MA: Beacon Press.

Parker, K. (2012). *The Boomerang Generation*. Washington, DC: Pew Social and Demographic Trends. Retrieved from: www.pewsocialtrends.org/2012/03/15/the-boomerang-generation/

Pillemer, K. and Suitor, J. J. (2002). Explaining mothers' ambivalence towards their adult children. *Journal of Marriage and Family*, 64(3): 602–613.

Pillemer, K., Suitor, J. J., Mock, S. E., Sabir, M., Pardo, T. B. and Sechrist, J. (2007). Capturing the complexity of intergenerational relations: Exploring ambivalence with later-life families. *Journal of Social Issues*, 63(4): 775–791.

Sassler, S., Ciambrone, D. and Benway, G. (2008). Are they really mama's boys/daddy's girls? The negotiation of adulthood upon returning to the parental home. *Sociological Forum*, 23(4): 670–698.

Scabini, E., Marta, E. and Lanz. M. (2006). *The Transition to Adulthood and Family Relations*. Hove: Psychology Press.

Seiffge-Kenke, I. (2013). "She's leaving home . . ." Antecedents, consequences, and cultural patterns in the leaving home process. *Emerging Adulthood*, 1(2): 114–124.

Settersten, R. A. (1998). A time to leave home and a time never to return? Age constraints on the living arrangements of young adults. *Social Forces*, 76(4): 1373–1400.

Settersten, R. A. and Ray, B. (2010). What's going on with young people today? The long and twisting path to adulthood. *The Future of Children*, 20(1): 19–41.

Smelser, N. J. (1997). The rational and the ambivalent in the social sciences: Presidential address. *American Sociological Review*, 63(1): 1–16.

Stone, J., Berrington, A. and Falkingham, J. (2014). Gender, turning points, and boomerangs: Returning home in young adulthood in Great Britain. *Demography*, 51(1): 257–276.

Umberson, D. (1992). Relationships between adult children and their parents: Psychological consequences for both generations. *Journal of Marriage and Family*, 54(3): 664–674.

Utley, T. (2016, April 29). Short of taking him to court, how can I make my darling baby boy (aged 24½) leave home? *Daily Mail*. Retrieved from: www. dailymail.co.uk/debate/article-3564808/TOM-UTLEY-asks-Short-taking-court-make-darling-baby-boy-aged-24-1-2-leave-home.html

White, N. R. (2002). "Not under my roof!" Young people's experience of home. *Youth and Society*, 34(2): 214–231.

Willson, A. E, Shuey, K. M. and Elder, G. H. (2003). Ambivalence in the relationship of adult children to aging parents and in-laws. *Journal of Marriage and Family*, 65(4): 1055–1072.

Wister, A. V., Mitchell, B. A. and Gee, E. M. (1997). Does money matter? Parental income and living satisfaction among 'boomerang' children during co-residence. *Canadian Studies in Population*, 24(2): 125–145.

4 Parents and co-resident graduates

Financial arrangements, responsibility and independence

Introduction

As we have seen, the parental home and parental support can provide a crucial safety net for graduates who have lived away from home during their undergraduate studies. In England and the United States, high proportions of young people move away from home to go to university.[1] As Sage et al. (2013) found in their study of students who left one English university between 2001 and 2007, migration histories tend to be complex and precarious with a heavy reliance on the parental safety net. Similarly in the US, one study found that 46 per cent of those who lived in colleges returned home on completion of their studies (Mulder and Clark, 2002). Parental resources played an important role in the likelihood of returning, providing support for the 'feathered nest' hypothesis, namely that young adults are more likely to return to a comfortable home (as the last chapter showed) (Avery et al., 1992; Mulder and Clark, 2002). A survey carried out by the Pew Research Center found that 42 per cent of college graduates under 30 were living with their parents or had done so temporarily in recent years (Parker, 2012). Other research has also found moving home after finishing full-time education to be a common occurrence (South and Lei, 2015).

On their return home from university, graduates may resume living as they had been before they moved away, not only in respect of their behaviour in the household (see Chapter 3), but also with parents acting as "providers" and paying the costs of their upkeep. Alternatively, parents may feel that such arrangements are no longer appropriate and may decide that their young adult children should be asked to contribute to the household economy. Indeed, this is how things *should be* according to some media, which has criticised the behaviour of parents for not charging their "boomerang" children rent which it is claimed would teach their children valuable life lessons. However, little research has addressed the reasons for arrangements that are put in place at the family level.

In this chapter, then, we focus on financial arrangements between parents and adult children and on how they relate to two notions we have discussed in previous chapters, namely responsibility and independence. The next section describes our approach and relevant literature; we also briefly outline our sample. We then explore financial arrangements including how they are negotiated and tensions – if any – that arise between parents and their adult children. Just as Chapter 3 showed that parents were able to articulate a firm obligation to provide "a safety net" for their graduate children, while at the same time reporting tensions – some severe – in their personal relationships, so this chapter reveals parental commitment to provide financial support, while also wanting to encourage financial responsibility. This also proved a source of tension for some, but on the whole parent/graduate relationships were characterised by fewer tensions over money than over behaviour in the familial home. Furthermore, there was evidence of more negotiations regarding financial arrangements, with mutually agreed outcomes[2] than, for example, with household work (see Chapter 3).

In analysing the arrangements, we also examine parents' and adult children's understandings of the notions of responsibility and independence and the ways in which parents sought to foster these in their young adult children. The final section discusses the findings.

Our approach

Psychological research literature has identified the importance of cognitive factors such as responsibility for one's self and making decisions as important markers of adulthood (Scheer et al., 1996). Thus, in his work with 'emerging adults' aged 20–29 years of age and young to midlife adults aged 30–55, Arnett has shown the importance of individualistic criteria for young adults achieving adulthood, including accepting responsibility for the consequences of one's actions and financial independence (Arnett, 2001). As we have seen, it was difficult for the graduates in our study to claim to be a fully independent adult while living in the family home. In this chapter, we interrogate in more depth the notions of both responsibility and independence in the context of the financial arrangements agreed – or imposed – by parents and their graduate children.

It is important to stress that independence can have different meanings and that these meanings vary over the life course. Qualitative sociological research by Ribbens (1994) focusing on mothers found that meanings underpinning the concept of independence for their children varied: they can be to do with content – such as self-care, or independent ideas, or to do with skills – such as decision-making and a future orientation. She stresses that children may need training or pushing towards independence.

Further qualitative sociological research has explored the notion of independence from the perspectives of parents and young people (Gillies et al., 2001). Interviews with 32 teenagers, the majority aged 17 to 18 years of age, 30 mothers and 31 fathers revealed that young people's understandings of independence entailed notions of behaving responsibly, trust between parents and children, and responsibility towards other family members. Young people also described how their parents helped them to develop skills to become more autonomous and learn independence. For both parents and teenagers, understandings of independence were 'shaped by a strong sense of connection to each other, conveyed in terms of mutual obligation, commitment and reliance' (Gillies et al., 2001: 18).

Both responsibility and independence are, as discussed in previous chapters, significant in the current study. However, financial independence, which can be seen as included within the broader concept of independence, is unlikely to be achieved immediately on graduation. Research carried out in the US found that around 65 per cent of parents expected to support their children financially for up to five years after college graduation; slightly more students also expected such support (Sallie Mae, 2015). As regards contributing to the family economy, research has found that young people do not necessarily pay for board and lodging when living in the parental home. One US survey found that nearly half of 25- to 34-year-olds who were living with their parents (or had done so in the recent past) paid rent (Parker, 2012; see also Sassler et al., 2008). In England, Sage et al. (2013) in a study of graduate returners from one university found that one-third had made a financial contribution to household costs. As we shall see, the reasons can vary.

Qualitative research has explored the reasons for making such contributions. Newman (2012: 118–119) cites the case of a family who required their adult daughter to help with her keep. The parents did not need the money but wanted to be reassured that their daughter was moving towards a 'productive life'. The mother stated 'you have to be a contributing member of this family, and you have to [contribute] at least two hundred dollars . . . it's not a free ride'. According to Newman, this is 'to inject some discipline into the relationship and makes it clear that there are rules', which in turn ties in with the issue of learning how to become financially independent, a topic frequently addressed in the media: 'Adult children will never become adults if they don't learn how to become financially independent from their parents' (Scott, 2015: 2). Other small-scale research carried out in the US has found that parents may not ask for contributions, so enabling their offspring to save (Warner et al., 2017).

It is also the case that financial transfers from parents to adult children are common. Significantly, these transfers are often targeted on the most needy, those who are younger, and those who are not working full-time (Kohli, 2004; Fingerman et al., 2009; Hartnett et al., 2012; Swartz et al., 2011). Qualitative research on the ways in which support is negotiated for young adults living at home has found that for English parents, "learning about responsibility" was the main factor determining how much parents should support their adult children, with too much support being associated with "spoiling" children. Significantly, the aim for many parents was 'that they should help children so that they could help themselves' (Holdsworth, 2004: 919).

On the basis of research that has been undertaken to date, we might expect that a range of different arrangements would be in place amongst our sample of co-resident graduates.[3] We might also expect parents to be seeking to foster responsibility and independence in their young adult children, albeit in different ways.

Financial arrangements

Our sample comprised 27 graduates and their parents (see Introduction). All parents had contributed towards (or paid in full) the costs of their children's undergraduate degrees. Six parents had in addition paid for postgraduate degrees or courses.[4] Graduates had lived with their parents for between three months and seven and a half years (mean 22 months). When they first returned to the parental home less than a quarter of graduates were employed and a similar proportion were unemployed (around a half were studying, in unpaid internships or volunteering). At the time of the interview, eight out of ten (22 graduates) were employed (three were studying, one was an unpaid intern and one was unemployed). The changes in employment status could be followed by modifications to the financial arrangements with the graduates' parents. In the following section, we explore the financial arrangements, and in so doing explore how parents sought to assist their children on the path to independence.

Financial arrangements varied between families. Most parents (20 out of 27) did not make co-residence conditional on specific financial arrangements. Only a minority of parents – less than a quarter – required their adult child to adhere to specific financial arrangements – whether contributing financially to the household economy by paying rent or by enforcing a savings scheme.

The reasons for making co-residence conditional varied, but tended to be associated with parents wanting to ensure that their children should demonstrate that they were responsible young adults. While the majority of parents did not make living in the family home conditional, their accounts of the financial arrangements revealed that they also often sought to inculcate responsibility and independence in their young adult children. These arrangements included both the provision of allowances and parents contributing to study costs. In other cases, children contributed in more *ad hoc* ways to the family economy.

In the following sections, we focus on three groups of families: first, families where in addition to providing board and lodging, parents provided financial assistance to their adult children (seven); second, families where parents provided board and lodging for their child which was not conditional on specific financial behaviours (13); and third, those families where parents made living in the family home contingent on their children either contributing to the family economy or saving money (seven).

Parents as providers of board and lodging plus financial support

In some families, parents were providing board and lodging and also giving their adult child financial support, either by means of a monthly allowance (four), or by financially supporting their children's studies (three). Allowances were generally a continuation of arrangements that had been established when the child was at secondary school, or more often at university. In two cases, parents had not stopped the direct debits to their children's bank accounts, indicating strong continuity with the past. In one of these families, the mother – who did not mention the allowance – stressed the importance of her daughter saving money so that she would be able to buy a property. In another, the daughter's responses suggested that she was still seen as a dependant by her parents, even though she indicated that she might have wanted more independence:

> My dad's not stopped the direct debit yet! I've told him he doesn't need to do it but I think they . . . have the view that they're . . . financially secure so if they can give me some money then they will do, so they don't need me to pay rent or such, so. I know some of my friends have to pay rent and things like that and I'm like 'oh I don't pay rent and my dad's giving me money', it's kind of a double thing.

One mother was worried that she might be spoiling her daughter but did not want to make life more difficult for her than it already was, so she retained and increased her allowance to pay for the family shopping: the daughter took responsibility for doing the shopping.

In other cases, parents had provided allowances to their children when they first returned to the parental home but had then stopped. In one such case, a mother stressed that she had done so as her daughter needed 'an income stream' which would be a step in the direction of greater independence. She felt that withdrawing the allowance would 'prompt her to get a job'. One graduate in this situation reported that she had to use her savings if she wanted to go and have a drink with her friends because she was not making any money and her parents were not giving her an allowance, unlike some of her peers. She was in full agreement with her parents' decision to stop her allowance:

> I don't want any of this. . . . I don't want my parents to have to support me, I just wish I had my own money. . . . I feel like I would like to be independent, I would like to have a job.

Independence in this case was strongly associated with paid work. Another graduate, whose parents had also stopped her allowance, needed 'not to be living at home'. She wanted a place of her own even though she felt that she had independence living in the parental home:

> My parents don't want me living at home, not in a nasty spiteful way but just because . . . they want me to be my own person and off making money and everything that comes part and parcel with all of that.

A very different situation arose in another case where the mother provided a 'top up' to her daughter's salary: her daughter had a casual, temporary contract and earned very little money. The mother provided a monthly allowance to help her with travel expenses and other costs and, in addition a credit card on her account which she had 'never, ever abused'. Once her daughter was in a permanent job, it had been agreed that she would contribute to her share of council tax (a local government property tax) as her mother felt that that she had a responsibility to do so: it was 'symbolic . . . of her being a separate person'.

In three families, parents financially supported children who were undertaking further study. In one case, parents had paid two-thirds of the fees for their daughter's master's degree. Although they felt that she should contribute to the costs as it would motivate her to work hard, they also wanted to help her because they did not want her savings account to be depleted. They had contributed to this account in the past to provide her with a 'little nest egg' to take care of educational expenses, and they had allowed their daughter to take control of the account at 18. She in turn had behaved responsibly and 'not plundered it'. As the father commented:

> We've always believed in teaching our children what they need to do but obviously there comes a point when they've got to make their

own decisions and you've just got to trust them and you just hope that you've done the right thing as they're growing up, and so far so good.

In another case, parents had loaned money to the daughter – they were contributing explicitly to further her education and enable her to become a lawyer. It had been agreed that she would pay back the loan when she had a permanent job. Her parents trusted her to do so and she had shared her accounting spreadsheets with her father.

Parents as providers of board and lodging

Around half the parents in our sample were providing board and lodging: they did not provide any regular financial support nor did they impose conditions relating to financial arrangements, such as charging rent. In some cases, parents explicitly saw themselves as "providers" so even when their children were earning they still saw themselves as responsible for them – as was the case before they went to university – and did not expect or want regular financial contributions to the family economy. This was the case for the seven families where at least one parent was of Asian origin. One father stressed that it was not the norm in Indian families for children to pay rent – this was part of the culture. Another father talked about the need for his children to learn to be responsible with regards to saving money for the future. He suggested that they should be 'investing in savings somewhere appropriate to cater for things . . . when we are not around'. Informal contributions to the household – such as buying food – were seen as learning about responsibility by putting the children 'on the ladder' until they were 'mature enough to go into their own nest'.

The notion of feeling not only responsible for oneself but also for family members was clearly exemplified by one graduate who wanted to 'set up' on his own:

> Once I'm on my own then I'll be supporting and helping them, and that's what I want to do and it's great because I can, because I don't pay any rent. . . . Because they support me at the moment it's given me the opportunity to grow much further than I could have if I was paying rent for example.

In this case the financial arrangements were – as the graduate saw it – hastening the time when he could be independent and provide support to his parents.

Where parents were from different cultural backgrounds, differences in cultural norms became apparent. In one case where the graduate was of mixed ethnicity, the South Asian mother felt that it was her responsibility to provide for her children. And in another case, the Asian father did not feel it appropriate for his daughter to contribute financially as he had not had to do so when he was younger; however, the mother who was White British felt that one of the ways of encouraging responsibility would be for her daughter to contribute to the household budget.

One White British father also wanted to be the "provider" and did not want his daughter to contribute to the household expenses even though she was earning: he did not need the money and wanted her to save for her forthcoming marriage.

While there was generally acceptance by graduates of these arrangements, there were occasional tensions between parents and co-resident children where the parent sought to be the provider. In one case, the graduate was not happy relying on her lone mother, who received no financial support from the father. She wanted to be independent, but as she said:

> I'm constrained by financial, career sort of limitations . . . any sort of feelings I have about lack of independence aren't really about moving back with my mum. It's about not having a job. If I had a job, it would make things a lot easier. I wouldn't feel so obligated to . . . rely on my mum so much and she could be relieved that she's not going to have to pay the bills.

The daughter thus wanted to take on more responsibility, but structural constraints – in particular not having a job – limited this possibility. In another case, the daughter, also wanted to contribute more to the family economy – and had the means to do so – but acknowledged that her father wanted to be the provider.

In some families, there were no such tensions. In one family, the parents worked together with their son to help him save money. The mother wanted him to 'amass as much savings as he can' and would rather he saved than give her money. She and her husband were active participants in their son's financial matters with the mother filing her son's bank statements and expenses and the father his tax returns.

In four families, adult children were earning very little money and this was one reason why parents did not ask for any financial contributions to the household economy. In such cases, responsibility could be fostered via different means – for example, the graduate having an obligation to do the shopping for the family. One mother commented that when her daughter was earning enough, she was thinking about instituting a savings scheme to teach her to budget for her living costs and also to help her save up for a property of her own. In this case, the mother saw independence as having to be learned with saving money being a way to foster this. Some parents felt that their children *should* contribute. One mother was from a working-class family and as a young adult she 'knew that she had to give up a portion [of her wages] to the household expenses'. Although her son was earning very little – and she and her husband did not expect him to contribute to the family economy – the mother felt young people should pay money towards their keep when living at home as it teaches them to be responsible, and she was also worried that she was spoiling her son.

Parents impose financial arrangements

In a minority of cases (seven), parents sought to inculcate responsibility by making co-residence contingent on their adult child making regular payments to them or requiring them to save money for the future. Thus, four graduates – all of whom were earning – made regular financial contributions to the family economy with the amount ranging from £100 to £400 a month. Three graduates were required to save money for the future.

The parents who required their children to contribute provided differing rationales. One father noted that when his daughter came back from university, the parents wanted her to pay a 'nominal' sum to get her used to the idea of paying something; the mother had subsequently increased the amount, although the father would have preferred to increase it further to give her 'a bit more consciousness about budgeting'. In another family, the mother said that she and her husband wanted to hold their daughter 'a bit more accountable as an adult'. They did not charge her rent initially, but after a year they decided that she needed to make a contribution; the spur had come from her husband, and following difficult negotiations she was now paying rent. In one case, the parents' motivation was to ensure that the son realised that 'life isn't a free ride really and you've got to pay your way in some way or other'. The son was perceived by his mother to have financial autonomy in that he had control over his finances:

> I think financially he's OK . . . but I don't think he's started paying off his student loan yet . . . that I'm leaving entirely to him. Unless he asks for advice, it's up to him now to sort out his finances.

One father stressed that there was an 'obligation now' for his son 'always to contribute'.

The graduates who made financial contributions accepted the arrangements. There were few tensions: some felt that they had an obligation to give their parents some money. The notion of fairness was invoked by three of the four who made such contributions. In one family, a norm had developed – the graduate's siblings had paid something so this 'seemed fair'. In another, the graduate's contribution covered the household's council tax and his food. This again, the graduate felt, was 'completely fair' and not expensive for what he got; nor did he mind, as he was earning money. In two families, the graduate's contribution to the family economy had increased. According to one graduate, she and her father had negotiated what was felt to be reasonable and so the amount had increased since she had been earning more.

While – as we have noted – graduates we interviewed were reported to be saving money, in three families, the fathers *required* their children to save money. In one case, this compulsory saving was construed as rent by father and daughter. The father – the family's 'financial officer' as he put it – decided that his daughter should give him one-third of her gross earnings each month. The father then put this money away in a separate account for a deposit for buying or renting a house. He and his wife wanted her to 'understand budgeting' – in short, that she would lose a third of her money to him, which is what she would pay if she were renting a property. He also wanted her to understand the amount she would have left if she were trying to live 'completely independently'. He pointed out that when she moved out she would need to pay for 'the . . . internet . . . gas, electricity, all utilities on top of rent'.

In a second case, the father did not want his daughter to 'get into the habit of spending' all her earnings once she started earning a good salary. Father and daughter agreed that she would not pay rent as neither was comfortable with the idea of her being a 'tenant', but that she should start saving and put two-thirds of her income in two accounts, one of which was for long-term savings and would be used for a house purchase at a later date. The father said: 'I think you need to be taught or told how to save or that you must save'.

In a third case, the parents did not discuss the possibility of their daughter paying rent when she initially moved back to the family home. However, her income increased over time and her father felt she should pay rent when she got a well-paid job. The daughter said that he joked about her 'not being able to live in the real world'. The father knew how much she was earning a month and, following explicit negotiations, it was agreed that she should make regular savings – the aim was to save money for a deposit on a flat.

The graduates who were required to save tended to be accepting of the arrangements that had finally been agreed. One graduate commented: 'He knows . . . how much I'm saving every month, and then every now [and then] he's like 'oh how is it going with the saving' and I'll be like 'oh I've got this much in the house account''. She also commented on her independence:

> I'm fully independent now. . . . I've got my own money, so I don't need to rely on my dad to give me money. . . . And if I need my parents, I can

fall back on them but I've got my own car, so I go anywhere I want, be fully independent.

She reported that her parents had set up 'various savings [schemes] for me over the years . . . and they help me manage that because I don't have a clue about how to invest money and make it work!' The notion of independence in this case related to having financial autonomy in the sense of not being reliant on her father for money; however, her father continued to manage her savings. Independence in this case did not include autonomy over all the graduate's financial matters.

Two of the graduates felt that their fathers did not need money from them: 'Bluntly, he doesn't need it. He's going to be paying the same . . . I use a bit more in terms of bills and obviously food'. Another felt that her father was not 'losing anything' and that she was 'just living' in the family as she was before. In these cases, the graduates were content to be dependent on their families and with the continuity this represented (see also Sassler et al., 2008).

In summary, all graduates who contributed to the household expenses considered the arrangements to be fair, with family norms often being invoked – for example, siblings having contributed in a similar way. The graduates who had agreed to save also accepted the arrangements.

Discussion and conclusion

This chapter set out to explore the financial arrangements between parents and graduate children and how parents sought to foster responsibility and independence – specifically financial independence – in their young adult children. As regards the financial arrangements, we identified three broad groups of parents: those who provided board and lodging and an allowance; those who provided board and lodging; and those who required their children either to save or to make financial contributions to the household economy.

Thus, some parents continued to give their adult children monthly allowances as they had done when they were younger, demonstrating continuity with the past; a degree of financial dependency on parents thus persisted. Some parents also provided financial support – via a gift or loan – if their children were undertaking further study. As previous research has found, parents viewed further study as worthy of financial support (cf. Fingerman et al., 2009). If adult children were unemployed or in precarious work, parents did not expect them to contribute to the family economy (see also Sassler et al., 2008). Some parents, particularly those where at least one was of Asian origin, regardless of whether their child was in work or not, saw themselves as providers. By way of contrast, some parents required their children to adhere to certain financial conditions when living in the family home: their adult child was required to make financial contributions to the household economy or to save money; these arrangements had sometimes been agreed once the child had secured employment.

In exploring the financial arrangements, we also examined understandings of the notions of responsibility and independence used by parents and young adults in their accounts, and the ways in which parents sought to teach their children about responsibility. As regards understanding of responsibility and independence, parents had different views. Financial independence was of paramount importance in attaining the status of adult in some cases. As one mother noted: 'She's not a child and yet she's not an adult, because to be an adult you need to have financial independence'. For others, the means to independence was via an income; as one father commented: 'You've got to have some income to be independent'. Different understandings of responsibility and independence were apparent amongst parents of Asian origin, who saw independence as being tied in with responsibility toward the family. This was exemplified by children making small contributions to the household. These findings resonate with those of Gillies et al. (2001: 16), who found Asian mothers linking their definition of independence with a broader sense of responsibility. Independence was interpreted as 'responsible conformity' rather than self-sufficiency. Asian parents in our study also tended to see independence as responsibility for oneself and towards other family members.

Many parents sought to inculcate responsibility and independence, albeit in different ways. The mother who was providing an allowance to her daughter who was in casual employment was enabling her daughter to get to work and cover her outgoings. However, another mother who also provided an allowance was concerned about spoiling her daughter, and the mother who withdrew her daughter's allowance was in effect incentivising her daughter to get a job. The parents who partially paid for their children's study costs could be seen to be fostering responsibility by requiring their young adult child to contribute to the costs.

While parents differed in how they felt that responsibility should be taught, learning about budgeting was a recurring theme. This was apparent amongst parents who encouraged savings and instituted savings schemes; they talked about awareness of and understanding budgeting. Learning about financial management was another element of responsibility. Saving money was a key feature in parents' accounts. One parent felt that his daughter was not living in the 'real world' and that saving money was a way of instilling responsibility as regards her financial behaviour. Another who imposed a savings scheme commented that his children could not live 'this kind of dream of earning what they earn which is not massive but having it always [as a] kind of free spend'. He let the daughter off a month's "rent" as he and his wife were going away and she had to 'look after house and cats, you know, be responsible'.

Saving could then be seen as a way of fostering responsibility and later independence along with understanding budgeting. It was often to assist with purchasing a property and so encouraging the graduate's departure from the family home. This echoes the work of Newman (2012: 121), who cites a young adult who had been living with his parents but was putting money into his savings to enable him to 'amass a nest egg' and 'give him a head start when he is out on his own'. Saving and understanding budgeting was part of learning to 'be responsible', resonating with research findings identifying responsibility for oneself as a key criterion for achieving adulthood (Arnett, 2001).[5]

Paying rent was also seen as a way of supporting children to learn to take responsibility for their finances and expenses. Indeed, one mother – whose son was earning very little and did not contribute to the household economy – felt that 'one of the ways of encouraging responsibility is to encourage contributing to the household budget'. She felt that she was spoiling her son and that he was not learning to be a responsible adult. This was echoed by another mother whose daughter did not contribute. Some parents felt that their child should contribute specifically to council tax which was again seen as a way of learning about responsibility. As one mother – whose daughter would pay council tax when she was in a better paid job – said that paying a share of the council tax was seen as 'symbolic of being a separate person'. The importance of acting responsibly as regards finances was exemplified by the mother who shared her credit card account with her daughter – she trusted her daughter to act responsibly with this. In other cases, adult children shared their accounting spreadsheets with their parents. Previous research has identified the importance of trust as part of the understanding of independence (Gillies et al., 2001).

Turning to young adults, independence had varied meanings – it could mean having a job, a flat, living separately from parents and freedom from parental support. It could be specifically associated with having an income, even if there were other constraints set by parents as to how earnings should be spent, as in the case of enforced savings. In this case financial autonomy – as regards decision-making – might be seen to be reduced, but nevertheless, the graduate *feels* independent (see also Manzoni, 2016; Mary, 2014).

The roles played by mothers and fathers differed, especially as regards the payment of rent and enforced savings. In short, the "management" of financial issues by parents appeared to be gendered, particularly with respect to fathers who saw themselves as providers, but also as "enforcers".

While mothers tended to encourage savings, and in some cases monitored them, it was fathers who enforced savings when they felt that their children were not behaving – or might not behave – responsibly with money. Financial control in these cases was an attempt to foster their children's progression toward financial responsibility and so adulthood. Ribbens (1994: 207) notes that in the private sphere of the family, the exercise of power can sometimes be understood as an expression of caring 'in order to further the interests of the children'. The role of father as provider also resonates with research by McCarthy et al. (2000) which found that it was fathers, not mothers, of dependent children who reported feeling responsible for providing for children's needs financially. This was not invariably the case in the present study, particularly with respect to divorced fathers: some of these financially supported their adult children, but others did not, causing financial difficulties for lone mothers without a secure income, and their children. This particular finding chimes with research demonstrating significantly lower levels of intergenerational transfers to adult children by divorced parents (White, 1992).

In conclusion, parents had different notions of responsibility and independence and different ideas about how this should be inculcated (see also Holdsworth, 2004). The approaches used differed between families – and could differ between parents in the same family too. For some parents, responsibility could be inculcated via their children making financial contributions to the household economy, or by smaller contributions to the household. For others, it could be by their child saving money for the future; where this did not happen voluntarily, it could be enforced by parents. Such saving was in order to facilitate moving out of the parental home at a later date and would also ensure that the adult child understood budgeting and living independently in the "big bad world". In the Asian families, specific cultural norms determined the financial arrangements. Responsibility could be inculcated by the adult child making small contributions to the household economy, but no payments by children to the household were expected. These specific norms appeared more uniform than in other families.

Notes

1 In 2011–12, 70 per cent of English-domiciled students on full-time three-year undergraduate programmes lived away from home (UK House of Commons, 2013). In the US, in 2012, 76 per cent of full-time students entering four-year colleges and universities reported that they planned to live in a college residence hall (Pryor et al., 2012).

2 See also West et al. (2016).

3 For a discussion of the nature of the negotiations – explicit or implicit (Finch and Mason, 1993) – see West et al. (2016).

4 See West et al. (2016) for details.
5 This contrasts with the view expressed by Warner et al. (2017) that not charging
rent absolves children of responsibility.

References

Arnett, J. J. (2001). Conceptions of the transition to adulthood: Perspectives from adolescence through midlife. *Journal of Adult Development*, 8(2): 133–143.

Avery, R., Goldscheider, F. and Speare, A. (1992). Feathered nest/gilded cage: Parental income and leaving home in the transition to adulthood. *Demography*, 29(3): 375–388.

Finch, J. and Mason, J. (1993). *Negotiating Family Responsibilities*. London: Routledge.

Fingerman, K., Miller, L., Birditt, K. and Zarit, S. (2009). Giving to the good and needy: Parental support of grown children. *Journal of Marriage and Family*, 71: 1220–1233.

Gillies, V., Ribbens McCarthy, J. and Holland, J. (2001). *'Pulling Together, Pulling Apart': The Family Lives of Young People*. London: Family Policy Studies Centre for Joseph Rowntree Foundation.

Hartnett, C., Furstenberg, F., Birditt, K. and Fingerman, K. (2012). Parental support during young adulthood: Why does assistance decline with age? *Journal of Family Issues*, 34(7): 975–1007.

Holdsworth, C. (2004). Family support during the transition out of the parental home in Britain, Spain and Norway. *Sociology*, 38(5): 909–926.

Kohli, M. (2004). Intergenerational transfers and inheritance: A comparative view. *Annual Review of Gerontology and Geriatrics*, 24(1): 266–289.

Manzoni, A. (2016). Conceptualizing and measuring youth independence multidimensionally in the United States. *Acta Sociologica*, 59(4): 362–377.

Mary, A. A. (2014). Re-evaluating the concept of adulthood and the framework of transition. *Journal of Youth Studies*, 17(3): 415–429.

McCarthy, J. R., Edwards, R. and Gillies, V. (2000). Moral tales of the child and the adult: Narratives of contemporary family lives under changing circumstances. *Sociology*, 34: 785–803.

Mulder, C. and Clark, W. A. V. (2002). Leaving home for college and gaining independence. *Environment and Planning A*, 34: 981–999.

Newman, K. S. (2012). *The Accordion Family*. Boston, MA: Beacon Press.

Parker, K. (2012). *The Boomerang Generation*. Washington, DC: Pew Social and Demographic Trends. Retrieved from: www.pewsocialtrends.org/2012/03/15/the-boomerang-generation/

Pryor, J. H., Eagan, K., Palucki Blake, L., Hurtado, S., Berdan, J. and Case, M. H. (2012). *The American Freshman: National Norms Fall 2012*. Los Angeles, CA: Higher Education Research Institute, UCLA.

Ribbens, J. (1994). *Mothers and Their Children: A Feminist Sociology of Childrearing*. London: Sage.

Sage, J., Evandrou, M. and Falkingham, J. (2013). Onwards or homewards? Complex graduate migration pathways, well-being, and the 'parental safety net'. *Population, Space and Place*, 19: 738–755.

Sallie Mae. (2015, May 19). *Teenagers and parents in agreement?* Retrieved from: http://news.salliemae.com/press-release/featured/teenagers-and-parents-agree ment-when-it-comes-preparing-college-answer-resoun

Sassler, S., Ciambrone, D. and Benway, G. (2008). Are they really Mama's boys/ Daddy's girls? The negotiation of adulthood upon returning to the parental home. *Sociological Forum*, 23(4): 670–698.

Scheer, S. D., Unger, D. G. and Brown, M. B. (1996). Adolescents becoming adults: Attributes for adulthood. *Adolescence*, 31(121): 127–131.

Scott, H. (2015, June 22). *Is it a big deal to let adult kids live at home rent free?* Retrieved from: http://theprovince.com/business/is-it-a-big-deal-to-let-adult-kids-live-at-home-rent-free

South, S. and Lei, L.(2015). Failures-to-launch and boomerang kids: Contemporary determinants of leaving and returning to the parental home. *Social Forces*, 94(2): 863–890.

Swartz, T. T., Kim, M., Uno, M., Mortimer, J. and O'Brien, K. (2011). Safety nets and scaffolds: Parental support in the transition to adulthood. *Journal of Marriage and Family*, 73: 414–429.

UK House of Commons. (2013, October 15). Written Answers, Hansard Vol. 568 col 684–685W.

Warner, E., Henderson-Wilson, C. and Andrews, F. (2017). 'It's give and take': Australian families' experiences of negotiating financial and domestic contributions when young adults return home. *Journal of Family and Economic Issues*. doi: 10.1007/s10834-017-9520-0

West, A., Lewis, J., Roberts, J. and Noden, P. (2016). Young adult graduates living in the parental home: Expectations, negotiations and parental financial support. *Journal of Family Issues*.

White, L. (1992). The effect of parental divorce and remarriage on parental support for adult children. *Journal of Family Issues*, 13(2): 234–250.

Concluding reflections

Introduction

Some influential literature has sought to emphasise intergenerational inequalities, as we saw at the beginning of this book, and has concluded that parents have done much better economically than their children can hope to do. At the same time, media accounts of contemporary transitions to adulthood have been dominated by fears that excessive "supervision" of students by their parents, and lengthy periods of co-residence on the part of graduates, will impede the transition to adulthood.

At the macro-level there are certainly structural impediments for young people nowadays that are different from those of their parents: increasing levels of student loan debt, the lack of affordable of housing and precarious employment. Nevertheless, at the micro-level our research shows that intergenerational relationships and exchanges are considerably more significant and complicated than some of the literature regarding intergenerational inequalities would suggest.

In this final chapter, we outline our key research findings and the central themes emerging from our study and conclude with comment on how our studies of predominantly middle-class young people and their parents raise as much fundamental concern about intragenerational as intergenerational inequality.

Our research findings

Earlier chapters present findings from our two research studies, each focusing on middle-class parents and their young adult children – students in the case of Chapters 1 and 2 and co-resident graduates in the case of Chapters 3 and 4. It is clear that parents tend to be aware that "things are different for their children" and to feel that they should help; this is reinforced by the degree of closeness between our samples of young adult children and their parents. The research reveals the centrality of family support for students and graduates: for both, financial subsidies and emotional support are crucial.

The parents were able to draw a sharp distinction between their experiences as students and those of their children. As students, virtually all the parents had received means-tested grants to support their living costs. Their children were required to pay tuition fees, and means-tested government loans had largely replaced grants to help cover living costs. The majority of parents provided regular financial contributions to their children, with the more affluent being able to pay the higher education costs in full or in part, or put money aside for future property purchases for their children. This was not a possibility for the less affluent parents in our sample, some of whom experienced financial strain and who on occasion were reliant on their children for financial support. There was also frequent contact between students and their parents, much more than the latter had had as students with their own parents. Students were on the whole less ambivalent about contact than the parents, who wanted to maintain close family ties but also to promote independence, and who did not want to interfere but nevertheless did not always exhibit behaviour that reflected this. The "lure of home" was much stronger for the students than it had been for their parents when they were at university. Parents tended to be more worried than were the students about possible return after graduation.

Graduates were also more sanguine about the return home than parents, who felt a strong obligation towards their young adult children but were anxious about the likely duration and how to deal with it. Very few set financial conditions – requiring their children to make financial contributions to the household or to save money. While some of the co-resident graduates were earning, their income was not in most cases sufficient to enable them to move out immediately. Some co-resident graduates "regressed" and behaved much as they had done as teenagers, which parents tended to find difficult; however, there was little evidence of negotiation until things reached a crisis point. Overall, there was more anxiety on the part of parents than graduates regarding co-residence – with uncertainty about the future. A central issue for graduates was finding a job, which was important for the graduate's sense of self as well as economic independence. This could also be a source of great parental anxiety and tension between parent and graduate. However, some parents were willing to support extensive job searches, and familial support could also enable graduates from more affluent families to wait until the "right job" came along. Parents sought to inculcate responsibility and it was hoped subsequent independence through different routes, in particular, contributing to household work, learning to budget and manage their finances, saving money, paying rent or enforcing saving schemes, with explicit negotiations regarding financial contributions or enforced saving being undertaken.

Transition to independence and adulthood

Our research contributes to the literature on the transition to independence and adulthood. Much research has been quantitative in nature but our qualitative studies and the "day-to-day" accounts we used show the difficulties of measuring concepts important in the transition, such as "satisfaction" or "dissatisfaction". Furthermore, investigation at the level of the family can reveal some important issues regarding both the societal level, in particular the implications of "privatisation to the family", as regards the changes to the funding of higher education in England, and the micro-level of changes in patterns of relationships and support between parents and young adult children.

Both the students and graduates in our samples were "semi-autonomous" (Goldscheider, 1985) or "semi-dependent" (e.g., Ahier and Moore, 1999) but in different ways. Most of the students were financially dependent. However, those in receipt of high levels of government financial aid with no regular financial support from parents felt financially independent, while those reliant on parents tended to feel independent in that they were exercising autonomous control over their money. However, socially the students enjoyed considerable freedom and independence. On the other hand, while some of the graduates earned enough to feel independent, the vast majority felt socially constrained by co-residence. Thus the transition to adult independence was not only longer and non-linear (Leccardi, 2016), but fluctuated in terms of the type of independence or autonomy that could be exercised.

Our findings indicate that both psychological and sociological research is important to understanding the transition, given the role played by individual and societal factors in this process. As Manzoni (2016) has pointed out, the concept of independence is multi-dimensional, involving living arrangements, earnings, financial support, self-perceived independence and a sense of being an adult. This usefully combines both the structural indicators used by sociologists (e.g., Furstenberg et al., 2004; Settersten and Ray, 2010) – to which we would add for our samples changes in policy affecting higher education funding and financial support and student loan debt levels – with the individualistic indicators used by psychologists (e.g., Arnett, 2001), among which "taking responsibility" and "establishing a relationship with parents as an equal adult" bulked large in our research.

More students felt confident about progress towards independence than did graduates, although students tended to use indicators related to greater self-perceived autonomy than structural independence – for example, deciding how best to manage or spend their parental allowance or government maintenance loan. Graduates tended to invoke more structural indicators, for example, getting a "graduate job", which was often difficult to find or moving out of the family home and living independently. But both students and graduates looked for changes at the household level, particularly in terms of a more "adult relationship" with their parents, to measure their progress towards independence and adulthood. Parents of both students and graduates tended to be more ambivalent about their children's transition to adulthood. Where the young adult children often saw themselves acting in more autonomous ways in respect of budgeting and spending, decision-making and relationships with parents, parents often saw continued dependence on their emotional support, with some expressing concern about their lack of responsibility both within the family home, and as regards their management of their financial affairs.

Furthermore, parents and adult children revealed in their accounts different understandings of key indicators of independence, particularly of "taking responsibility". For example, parents wanted graduates to take more responsibility in their households, but the latter did not necessarily recognise a relationship between contributions to household work and developing independence. The existing literature tends not to acknowledge the complicated and different understandings of autonomy and independence, and the tensions that may arise from them.

There were therefore tensions between parents and young adult children not only in terms of how they interpreted progress towards adulthood, but also in their day-to-day lives. Nevertheless, most striking is the close contact between parents and children, and the support provided by parents. Indeed, there is evidence in many cases that the achievement of adult independence had become a "family project" (Kohli and Albertini, 2008), particularly for those graduates for whom the aims of another period of co-residence were primarily to have the time to apply for the type of graduate job they really wanted, and to be able to save money in order to move out. However, parents of graduates could be concerned that their comfortable homes might prove to be a disincentive to achieving full independence. Parental contact with student children could be intense, and while there was little evidence of the kind of overparenting referred to as "helicoptering", there was plenty of evidence of extensive emotional and financial support.

The existing literature stresses the importance of greater involvement on the part of parents "enabling autonomy" (Gillies et al., 2001; Soenens et al., 2007; Wartman and Savage, 2008). Day-to-day, the evidence for this is mixed, for students and for graduates, despite parental concern to promote autonomy and independence. But in the longer term, parental support may be important for student adaptation to at least a semi-dependent lifestyle and the opportunities for graduates to take the time to apply for and get a "good job". Nevertheless, it could be a challenge for parents to offer support for autonomous behaviour on the part of their young adult children, rather than respond to the child's expressed or perceived needs in a manner that might delay independence. Taken together, the time at university and another, unspecified period of co-residence has extended the transition to adulthood and has carried with it different dimensions of dependence, autonomy and independence. The norms for managing elongated transition are in many cases yet to come clear.

Concluding thoughts

It is important to note that both our studies focused on middle-class families and the relationships between parents and their young adult children, and that the relationships were such that both parents and adult children were willing to participate in the research. While our samples of parents and young adults were not designed to be representative of the respective populations of students and co-resident graduates, there was nevertheless heterogeneity within our samples. This was especially clear as regards the nature of the financial support provided by parents to their young adult children – particularly students – and also in respect of the determination of parents to support their young adult children emotionally.

In recent decades, a range of structural macro-level changes have taken place affecting young adults in England. The government has replaced student grants with student loans and universities have started charging tuition fees, which students are required to pay – directly or indirectly via government loans – to universities; these have increased over time. University education has been positioned as a private investment (cf. Wyn and Woodman, 2006) and has essentially been "privatised to the family". Furthermore, housing costs have increased and employment has become more precarious. At the micro-level of the family, parents have stepped in where they can to support their young adult children. More affluent parents are able to protect their children in various ways and are thus able to "transmit" their financial advantages to their children as is made particularly clear in our study of students and parents.

Willetts (2010: 253) claimed that 'younger generations are losing out', but as Macnicol (2015: 159) notes: 'Within one generation [there is] considerable heterogeneity and many inequalities', including class, ethnicity, wealth and educational status. Our evidence suggests that a key dividing line in the future is likely to be between those in the younger generation who are with and without familial economic resources (see also Hood, 2017). The cleavages between young people from more and less affluent families are likely to remain. In 2012–13, university tuition fees in England increased up to £9,000 per annum. Interest rates on student loans have also increased. And while means-tested loans are available to help with living costs, the Conservative government abolished maintenance grants for low-income students from 2016–17. It is thus clear that student loan debt will remain the highest for those from low-income families (see Callender and Mason, 2017).

Families who are able to offer financial support to students and accommodation to graduates, sometimes for several years, can ease the burden of student loan debt and also help their young adult children to find their way into the labour market, sometimes via unpaid internships, and into housing, whether shared and rented, or owned. Consequent intragenerational inequalities will in all likelihood increase in future years with increasing "privatisation to the family" in the field of higher education. Private family resources – material and non-material – will undoubtedly continue to provide a buffer for young adult children against the structural and policy changes thrust upon them.

References

Ahier, J. and Moore, R. (1999). Post-16 education, semi-dependent youth and the privatisation of inter-age transfers: Re-theorising youth transition. *British Journal of Sociology of Education*, 20(4): 515–530.

Arnett, J. J. (2001). Conceptions of the transition to adulthood: Perspectives from adolescence through midlife. *Journal of Adult Development*, 8(2): 133–143.

Callender, C. and Mason, G. (2017). Does student loan debt deter higher education participation? New evidence from England. *The Annals of the American Academy of Political and Social Science*.

Furstenberg, F., Kennedy, S., McLoyd, V. C., Rumbaut, R. G. and Settersten, R. A. (2004). Growing up is harder to do. *Contexts*, 3(3): 33–41.

Gillies, V., McCarthy, J. and Holland, J. (2001). *"Pulling Together, Pulling Apart": The Family Lives of Young People*. York: Joseph Rowntree Foundation.

Goldscheider, F. and DaVanzo, J. (1985). Living arrangements and the transition to adulthood. *Demography*, 22(4): 545–563.

Hood, A. (2017, April 23). *Seven reasons it helps to have rich parents*. Retrieved from: www.bbc.co.uk/news/uk-39519844

Kohli, M. and Albertini, M. (2008). The family as a source of support for adult children's own family projects: European varieties. In C. Saraceno (Ed.), *Families, Ageing and Social Policy: Intergenerational Solidarity in European Welfare State* (pp. 38–58). Cheltenham: Edward Elgar.

Leccardi, C. (2016). Facing uncertainty. Temporality and biographies in the new century. In C. Leccardi and E. Ruspini (Eds.), *A New Youth? Young People, Generations and Family Life* (pp. 1–14). London: Routledge. First edition (2006). Aldershot: Ashgate.

Macnicol, J. (2015). *Neoliberalising Old Age*. Cambridge: Cambridge University Press.

Manzoni, A. (2016). Conceptualizing and measuring youth independence multidimensionally in the United States. *Acta Sociologica*, 59(4): 362–377.

Settersten, R. and Ray, B. E. (2010). *Not Quite Adults*. New York: Random House.

Soenens, B., Vansteenkiste, M., Lens, W., Luyckx, K., Goossens, L., Byers, W. and Ryan, R. M. (2007). Conceptualizing parental autonomy support: Perceptions of promotion of independence versus promotion of volitional functioning. *Developmental Psychology*, 43(3): 633–646.

Wartman, K. and Savage, M. (2008). *Parental involvement in higher education: Understanding the relationship among students, parents and the institution*. Higher Education Report Series, 33(6). San Francisco, CA: Association for the Study of Higher Education.

Willetts, D. (2010). *The Pinch: How the Baby Boomers Took Their Children's Future – and Why They Should Give It Back*. London: Atlantic Books.

Wyn, J. and Woodman, D. (2006). Generation, youth and social change in Australia. *Journal of Youth Studies*, 9(5): 495–514.

Index